Lynn McKay

SO NOW YOU'RE ON YOUR OWN

A positive approach for single parents

LYN HENLEY

BayBooks
An imprint of HarperCollins*Publishers*

The publisher has made every effort to ensure that all contact details were correct when this book went to print.

A Bay Books Publication

Bay Books, an imprint of HarperCollins*Publishers*
25 Ryde Road, Pymble, Sydney, NSW 2073, Australia
31 View Road, Glenfield, Auckland 10, New Zealand

First published in 1994.

National Library of Australia
Cataloguing-in-Publication data:

Henley, Lynette.
    So Now You're On Your Own
    ISBN 1 86378 174 9

1. Single parents — Life skills guides. I. Title.
306.856

Printed in Australia by Griffin Paperbacks

10 9 8 7 6 5 4 3 2 1
98 97 96 95 94

Acknowledgement

Material in this book has been adapted from publications of the Department of Social Security, with their permission. Although all such information was correct at the date of publication, it is subject to alteration with legislative and policy changes.

Contents

Look back just long enough to learn from your mistakes.

Look forward just long enough to dream but

live today, because it is the foundation

of the rest of your life.

(DOUGLAS RICHARDS, I'M ON THE WAY TO A BRIGHTER DAY,
BLUE MOUNTAINS PRESS, COLORADO, 1984.)

Try Your Wings

Mary Kay Cosmetics awards its high achievers bumble bee pins in gold and diamond. I asked a director with Mary Kay what the significance of the bumble bee was. She replied 'aerodynamically, it should be impossible for the bumble bee to fly but no-one told the bumble bee'. You will often be told what you cannot do, what is beyond your reach. You will rarely be told what you can do and what is within your reach. Try your wings. The worst that can happen is that you won't take off. The best that can happen is that you will fly.

So now you are on your own or contemplating sole parenthood as an option. Whichever it is, you are more than likely to be on an emotional roller coaster which will cloud your judgement and impede your capacity for rational decision-making.

You face what appears to be a never-ending list of problems and decisions, which probably includes:

• Where are you going to live?
• How are you going to pay the bills?
• Where can you get a job?
• Who can help care for the children?
• What do you do about child maintenance?
• What subsidies or allowances are you eligible for?
• Who can help with family problems and conflicts?

The list never seems to end. No sooner have you worked your way over, under or around one problem than another looms large on the horizon. There is no one to take you by the hand and lead you through the maze of sole parenthood or give you a reassuring hug and tell you that it will all work out in the end. You cannot even see the end. There appears to be just one long tunnel, where someone forgot to turn on the lights. So there you are, fumbling around in the dark, tripping over obstacles in your way. If only someone would turn on the lights, you would be OK.

Well, don't stand around waiting for someone to do it for you.

The caretaker went home and won't be back. You have to find the switch all by yourself.

You have learnt the first lesson of sole parenthood: you are it. But take heart. You are not on your own. There are thousands of people in the same situation. 'So what?' you say. 'That's cold comfort if we are all fumbling about in the dark.'

Time for the second lesson in sole parenthood: take some positive action.

There is a large network of government and private agencies ready, willing and able to provide you with all the support you can use. All you have to do is plug into the network. How? Now that is a good question.

There is no one person or agency that has all the information or can answer all your questions. If you need to find an address, you get out your street directory, look up the suburb, find the appropriate street, note the map number and reference points and you know where you need to go. No such luck with the state of sole parenthood.

As a result of this realisation and having spent quite a time fumbling around a dark tunnel myself, I have put together this book to provide relevant information, answers to some questions and directions about where to obtain others.

Sole parenthood is not always easy but then nothing worthwhile ever is. You can make of your sole parent status what you will. You can sit back, feel sorry for yourself, blame the system and everyone else for your circumstances, which I admit having done. Or you can take some positive action, plug into the system and make it a positive, worthwhile journey of self-discovery. The choice is yours.

Introduction

- There are two basic truths of sole parenthood.
- The first is — you are it.
- You will rise, fall, stall or stagnate according to choices you make or allow others to make for you.
- The second is — take some positive action.

You and only you can effect changes in your life. Others can provide advice and information on how you could possibly proceed but the bottom line is that you have to act upon that advice before it can have any impact.

If you are not prepared to accept responsibility for your circumstances or take some positive action and follow through, don't bemoan your fate and blame the rest of the world. Place the blame firmly where it belongs, with yourself.

This book aims to provide general information on which you can act, if you choose, and advice on where to go for further information. Perhaps this book may reduce the time it takes to find your way around the system and get your life moving in a new and rewarding direction.

Sole parenthood may result from separation or divorce, or from the illness, the imprisonment or even the death of your partner. Regardless of how you arrive at this state, the obstacles and challenges are basically the same.

I have attempted to be non-sexist in writing this book as men are also sole parents. I even started to write a chapter devoted to sole fathers. However, the problems faced by sole fathers, in my opinion, are basically the same as those faced by sole mothers. Most government and private support groups do not differentiate between male and female sole parents. I would say, however, that state governments rarely, if ever, have a department devoted to men's affairs as they do to women's. There are probably more government-funded agencies providing advice and assistance to women who are seeking employment or re-entry to employment than there are providing similar advice and assistance to men. However, this does not alter the fact that the difficulties are basically the same.

The content of this book has been put together from personal experience, the experiences of other sole parents, information and advice received from various government departments, State and Commonwealth, support agencies, literature from a wide variety of sources, friends, family, and acquaintances. The list is extensive. Without diminishing the contribution made by many, I would like to single out a few people for a special mention: my parents and family, for being supportive but ensuring that I stood on my own two feet; De'arne, who not only listened, supported and never gave up on me but kept reinforcing the need to take action, to be a 'doer' rather that a 'gonna doer', until it finally sank in; Christine, who was not only instrumental in getting the manuscript to the publisher but held the fort while I wrote it; the staff at the Department of Social Security's Media and Liaison Office in Perth, who were more than cooperative in providing information and useful contacts.

Taking Control of Your Life

If you are anchored to the past, you will bob around on your mooring and your movement in any direction will be restricted by the length of the anchor rope. You need to put the past where it belongs, behind you.

Well, now we get to the bottom line—what you can do about yourself to help yourself. No one knows better than I that knowing what you should do and actually doing it are two very different matters. I was queen of the procrastinators. I had an infinite list of excuses for not doing what I knew I should and I could rationalise every one of them. I had read a lot of books on increasing self-esteem, assertiveness, motivating yourself, and so on. I knew what I needed to do but it was the doing that was the problem. I was suffering from terminal procrastination.

So what changed for me? How did I take control of my life? It wasn't easy. I moved forward, I slipped backwards and I stalled.

The key, for me, came down to a difference in definition. The Oxford Dictionary defines 'to procrastinate' as 'to put off doing things, leave things undone as long as possible'. This is the generally accepted definition of procrastinate.

The opportunity arose for me to become involved in selling a product. It was a good opportunity, so I decided I needed to do some revision on my selling skills. I took out my Tom Hopkins tapes and sat down to listen to them once again. Tom Hopkins is one of the world's most successful sales trainers. One of the problems he dealt with was what he called the 'Dirty Dozen Stressors'. Procrastination was one of these. His definition of procrastination was 'living yesterday, avoiding today, thus ruining tomorrow'. For me the light bulb flickered. There was a brief moment of illumination. My life did not turn around at that precise moment but the key to making the change had been inserted in the lock. I began to take the steps necessary to turn that key. It was a long hard haul. As I have said, I moved forward, I slipped backwards and I stalled. I still slip backwards occasionally, I still stall sometimes but, overall, I move forward. What follows are the steps I took to gain control.

TAKING RESPONSIBILITY

Taking responsibility means that you don't blame other people or bad luck when things in your life are not as you want them to be. You accept responsibility for the consequences of your choices. Whether your choices are active (you make a definite choice), or passive (you allow others to make the choice for you), you are responsible for them and their consequences.

I have found that those who fail to take responsibility for their lives usually fall into one of two categories. They are either 'casualties' or 'good samaritans'.

Casualties are those who live in a constant state of misery. They can rarely find any facet of their lives to be happy about and, just when things appear to be going well, some disaster strikes. Nothing is ever their fault.

Good samaritans are those who always have a solution to your problems. More often than not, they are caring people who have difficulty saying 'no'. They usually put the needs of others before their own and sometimes complain that they have no time for themselves.

Although these personality types appear to be very different, their behaviour has a common result. The casualties gain attention for their 'woes' and it is not their fault that things don't change. The good samaritans gain attention for their 'good deeds' and are too busy to deal with their own problems and effect changes in their lives. Both behaviour patterns are attention-seeking and designed to avoid change.

You may move from being a casualty to being a good samaritan and convince yourself that you have taken a step towards taking control of your life. What you have done, however, is to swap one attention-seeking behaviour pattern for another. In effect, you are no closer to taking responsibility for your life or gaining control of it.

The only way to take responsibility is to stop making excuses. Stop looking for people or events you can blame. Accept that you are ultimately responsible for yourself and your life choices. In other words, become self-directed.

LEARNING TO LOVE YOURSELF

This one can be really tough. Your image of yourself is developed during your lifetime and is affected by your circumstances and relationships. It's easy to love yourself and feel comfortable with who you are when everything in your life is going well and you are happy with how you look. It's not so easy when relationships fail, you put on weight, lose a job, or suffer a financial reversal. However, these are the times when you need to love yourself the most, to have a good self-image and high self-esteem.

How often have you heard the comment 'she loves herself' or 'he loves himself' used in a negative way to describe someone who is arrogant, selfish, uncaring or rude? You have probably lost count.

Acknowledging that you deserve the best life has to offer, liking yourself and being able to look in the mirror and say 'I love you' at any time in your life is self-love. It is being able to accept a compliment graciously.

We often look to others for acceptance and approval, to our parents, partners, friends and children. Acceptance and approval come from within. Your own approval is all you need. Accept that it is alright to be less than perfect and to make mistakes. You are only human, after all. You are under no obligation to measure up to the expectations of others, just as they are not required to measure up to yours. Treat yourself gently, as you would a good friend: with patience, consideration and respect.

Developing a good self-image involves consciously changing the way you see yourself. Start by acting like the person you want to be. Your style of dress or hairstyle is probably easiest to change. Changing your shape may take longer and a more concerted effort. Some images you have of yourself are not as easily changed as your appearance. These are the ways you have learned to think of yourself. You may see yourself as being unassertive or a failure in a specific area of your life. These images have been developed over a period of time and you may need to seek help in changing them. You could attend counselling sessions privately, join a self-help or support group or take a course. Whatever you choose to do, it must move you closer to the image you want to create.

You may not have made the active choices which resulted in your self-image but you can certainly make active choices which will change it. It won't happen overnight and it won't happen simply because you want it to. It will happen gradually and it will happen if you take some action.

LETTING GO

If you are anchored to the past you will bob around on your mooring and your movement in any direction will be restricted by the length of the anchor rope. You need to put the past where it belongs, behind you.

This is not always easy, quite often painful and may involve seeking help from a qualified professional. It involves facing up to emotions you have buried and never dealt with. You have to let go of the anger and resentments you may have spent years acquiring. You have to face up to your feelings of guilt and acknowledge their cause. You have to forgive yourself.

Your life is not going to turn around miraculously and move ahead at full speed because you manage to let go of the past and draw up the anchor. Nevertheless, you will have set the climate to enable you to make change and move forward with confidence.

One method I found particularly effective was to write to the people with whom I was angry or against whom I bore some real or imagined resentment. I wrote those letters as if I were actually talking to those people. I said all the things I was not able to say to them face-to-face. Once written, I drew two lines across each page, as if crossing a cheque, and wrote 'I have dealt with this'. I then took the letters and burnt them. Admitting the anger and expressing it safely was very cathartic. Burning those pages not only destroyed the letters but was a physical letting-go. It may not work for everyone but it did for me.

Look back just long enough to learn from your mistakes. Look forward just long enough to dream but live today, because it is the foundation of the rest of your life.

GETTING POWER

What is your concept of a powerful person? Perhaps it is someone with the money to live their life as they choose. It may be someone who is able to influence the lives of others. It may be someone with a strong personality. It could be any combination of these and include other traits not mentioned.

Making decisions and acting upon them is powerful. Nothing has ever been achieved without someone first making a decision and then acting upon it. You have the power to make of your life what you choose, to become self-directed. You don't have to wait to be empowered. You can grab power for yourself.

If you were to take a close look at the powerful people you know, you would find they all have one thing in common. They are self-directed people. They make decisions and then act upon them. They choose their own direction. They don't wait for someone else to make a decision and then make the best of how it affects them.

The choice is yours. You can grab power for yourself and move in the direction of your choice or drift with the currents created by those who do.

DEVELOPING A POSITIVE ATTITUDE

Your attitude to yourself, your family, your work and your friends determines your level of achievement is these areas. If your attitude is negative, always expecting the worst, looking for faults and shortcomings, you will get what you expect. The worst will happen and you will constantly find things to complain about with friends, family, work, in fact all aspects of your life. You will go through life sabotaging any chance you may have of a happy and rewarding existence.

If, on the other hand, you have a positive attitude to all aspects of your life, you expect the best it has to offer and look for the strengths and virtues in family and friends, you will find friends, family and even your boss have commendable personality traits and behaviour patterns. Because you are no longer sabotaging yourself, the better things in life will come to you.

Your attitude is reflected in the way in which people respond to you. If you are optimistic, always expecting the best life has to offer, people will respond favourably and want to be around you. If you are pessimistic, always expecting the worst, people will just as soon avoid you.

Being negative and miserable is a habit. Being positive and happy is a habit. Why, then, choose to be negative and miserable?

To develop a positive attitude, you need to redefine your language and the way in which you look at things.

For example, take the accepted concept of 'winning'. This does not necessarily mean coming first. You win when you have attempted something and given it your best. You win when you get what you want—not what your mother, father, children, partner, brother, sister or friends want for you but what you want for yourself. Look at the accepted definition of failure: 'an unsuccessful person or thing'. You are not a failure if you don't make it. You only fail if you didn't try hard. When things don't go the way you plan, don't concentrate on what you did wrong. Give yourself a pat on the back for what you did right.

Every negative thought impacts on your attitude. Every sound that goes in the ear ends up in the brain. Negative talk from others impacts on your attitude. Concentrate on surrounding yourself with positive people. If necessary, do as I did. I told friends and family I was concentrating only on the positive aspects of my situation and I chose not to discuss the negative ones. If they brought them up in conversation, I told them I did not choose to talk about them and changed the subject. It took some time but eventually they realised the futility of raising them. Not discussing them with others greatly diminished their impact on my attitude to life.

Concentrate on thinking positive thoughts. Several years ago I read or heard the saying, 'the thoughts we choose to think are the tools we use to paint the canvas of our lives'. We all have that person who sits inside our head, is quick off the mark with criticism and never fails to let us know what we have done wrong or point out the negative aspects of our situation. It is hard not to listen when it speaks to us but ignore it you must. I refused to listen. When that little voice started up I would hum, sing to myself or make myself think of a pleasant time in my life. I only chose to listen to it when the conversation was positive. It took some time but now my voice rarely has anything negative to say. It has finally come to the realisation that I will ignore it and no one likes to be ignored.

One exercise I found effective in handling negative thoughts and emotions was to carry a notebook with me and, when I felt discouraged, upset, worried or afraid, I would write down what was making me feel that way. I would set a time within the next 24 hours to sit down and handle the problem. Acknowledging the problem and making an appointment to deal with it meant that I didn't have to think about it again until the appointed time. To counteract negative thoughts and emotions, I would write down two positive thoughts, two things I could feel encouraged, calm and confident about.

When I focused on the positive aspects of my life, more often than not, I found that the choices I made yielded positive results. You cannot eliminate the negatives from your life altogether but, by refusing to let them become the focus of your life, you can greatly diminish their impact.

RESPOND, DON'T REACT

At first glance, there does not seem to be much difference between 'responding' and 'reacting' to a situation. Both involve an action or answer in response to stimuli. The real difference lies in the type of action taken. A reaction is a more reflex or uncontrolled action. A response is a more controlled and considered action.

If you are reactionary, as I was, taking control of your actions is difficult, if not impossible. You may have set yourself a direction to follow and, when you encounter the first obstacle, you react. It is a reflex action. You haven't stopped to consider its ramifications and, as a result, you may discover that you have changed direction. Now you have to waste time and effort to redirect yourself and make up lost ground. It may even be too difficult to redirect yourself, so you make the best of the direction in which you are heading and continue up that path. If you had been responsive when that first problem was encountered, you would have stopped, considered the ramifications and then taken action which would have enabled you to keep to your original direction.

When we are in reactionary mode we are not choosing the direction in which we want to go. We are simply following the path to nowhere.

Making the change from being reactionary to being responsive is not all that difficult but it does take time and practice, particularly if you have a quick temper. Stop and think. Ask yourself, 'Can I achieve anything positive from this situation? If so, what do I want to achieve? If I cannot achieve a positive result, what action can I take to minimise any negative fallout?' Remind yourself that you have chosen to be self-directed, that you have the power to make a choice which will decide the outcome. Remind yourself that you choose not to bounce around, simply rebounding from one situation into another, that you choose to stop, think and respond.

One technique I found particularly useful was to talk to myself. When faced with a confrontation situation I would tell myself to keep my cool, not to get upset. If the other person wanted to, that was OK for them. I chose to stay calm and maintain control. If I found I was getting agitated, I would tell myself to ease back and loosen up. I concentrated on listening, actually hearing what was being said rather than anticipating what was going to be said.

A friend gave me a very valuable piece of advice. She told me that I couldn't go through life reacting to everything that happened to me. The frustration would eventually become too much. 'Don't be a sponge; be a non-stick fry pan', was her advice. It was excellent.

PROBLEM SOLVING

You may be wondering why problem solving is so far down my list. Surely it should be first. After all, if we could solve our problems effectively, life would be a breeze. However, before you can do so you need to develop the habit of being self-directed, making decisions and then acting upon them. You need to be able to define the problem clearly, look at all possible solutions, select the most appropriate, develop a plan of action and then put the plan into action.

Life's drifters generally don't solve their problems. More often than not, they don't admit to problems. 'Ignore them and they will go away' is their general philosophy. What happens, however, is that the problems become compounded by inaction and then appear to be too big to tackle. Have you ever heard the sayings, 'even an elephant can be eaten, one bite at a time' or 'the longest march started with the first step'? No problem is too big to solve. It may take time and careful planning but it can be overcome.

You need to organise your problem solving. It is best done when you have uninterrupted time available. You will need to have all information relevant to the problem on hand. You will need something to write on.

Defining Your Problem

Start by writing a definition of your problem and what you want from the situation. Some people confuse a conflict between possible solutions with the problem itself. They often become so involved in defending their solution that the problem is never defined. Concentrate on defining your problem in terms of what you want. It may be necessary to break large problems down into a series of smaller problems.

Once you have clearly defined the problem, you need to make a list of all possible ramifications.

Finding Solutions

Now you can turn your attention to thinking of solutions. The purpose of this exercise is to think up as many solutions as possible. You are going for quantity not quality, so write each one down, even if it seems silly. Avoid the temptation to evaluate solutions as you think of them.

When you have completed your list of possible solutions, work through them from first to last, noting next to each one all the advantages and disadvantages you can think of.

You can now choose a solution. The most expedient solution is not always the best. Perhaps it may be necessary to use a combination of two or more solutions to solve the problem.

Implementing Your Solution

Once you have chosen a solution to your problem, you need to plan exactly how you will implement it. Write down the steps you need to take. Until you write it down, you have not committed yourself to the plan.

Follow your plan through. Until you do, it is just a good idea. How many good ideas have you had that you never acted on?

If your solution worked, congratulations. If it didn't, what went wrong? Was the problem clearly defined? Do you need to try a different solution?

Yes, this method is time consuming, but it has several benefits. You are more likely to succeed in solving your problems and your attention is focussed on one problem at a time. I had a tendency to look at all my problems at once. The prospect of overcoming them all was so daunting that I gave up. By using this method, I was able to tackle my problems one at a time. As I solved the smaller ones successfully, I gained the confidence to take on the larger ones. I also found that there were some problems —those that really belonged to other people — that I could not solve but this method enabled me to find positive ways of coping with them.

OVERCOMING FEAR

The Oxford Dictionary defines fear as 'emotion caused by impending evil, alarm, dread'. Unless you overcome them, your fears will hold you firmly where you are.

We aren't born with our fears. We learn them. We are taught to be fearful of situations we cannot control. Our fears protect us from being hurt. If we don't strive to succeed we cannot suffer the pain of failure. If we don't put ourselves forward we cannot suffer the pain of rejection. If we don't succeed we don't have to cope with the results of success.

When we are immobilised by our fears, we are really saying that we lack trust in our judgements, opinions and abilities. People often comment on the apparent fearlessness of young children. It is not that they are exceptionally brave but that they trust that everything will be OK, that they will be looked after. They trust in abilities they are unaware they have. They haven't yet learned not to trust themselves or others.

We sometimes use our fears to construct a wall around us to insulate us from possible hurts and pains, to create a safe, comfortable haven, where nothing ventured means no pain. We terrify ourselves with thoughts of what might be, rather than finding out what is.

Acknowledging our fears for what they are—limitations created by our minds in order to protect us from possible hurt or pain—enables us also to create the antidote. You would consider it inane not to drive your car because it might break down, never to cross a road because you might get run down, not to apply for a job because you might not get it or not to buy a lottery ticket because you might not win. You realise that there are no guarantees but the risks are acceptable. Why, then, not strive because you might not succeed? Why stand back because you might be rejected?

Life isn't a laboratory experiment where the outcome can be guaranteed in a controlled environment. There are too many variable factors to guarantee a satisfactory outcome. No one can guarantee you will be rich and famous, happy and healthy or successful and prosperous. What can be guaranteed is that you won't be any of these if you don't strive or take some risks, if you don't overcome some of your fears and knock some holes in the wall.

Some of your fears you will be able to overcome by yourself. Some, you may need professional help and advice to master. Accept that the outcome will be determined not by what happens to you but by how you cope with those events. Accept that you will always feel fear. As long as you grow and undergo changes in your life, the fear will not go away. The only way to overcome it is to do what you fear. Confront your fears by choice. Fear is generally caused by anticipation. The longer you spend thinking rather than doing, the greater the fear becomes. When we back away from our fears and allow them to dominate us, we generally feel despondent, depressed, pessimistic and ineffective. When we reverse our behaviour and move toward our fears, we generally feel empowered, optimistic, effective and satisfied. The secret, therefore, of overcoming your fear is to do it and do it now.

'It is not because things are difficult that we do not dare. It is because we do not dare that they are difficult.'

YOU CAN BE WHO YOU WANT TO BE

Do you know who you want to be? Do you know what you want to achieve during your lifetime? Have you taken the time to look back on where you have come from and look forward to where you want to go? Probably not. We are generally so busy taking care of the serious business of life that we don't allow ourselves to dream. Contrary to popular opinion, what you want cannot wait until the serious business of life is taken care of, simply because the serious business of life is never taken care of.

Take the time now to find out who you want to be and what you want to achieve. Imagine yourself at 95, sitting in your rocking chair on the front verandah. You are gently rocking back and forth, looking back on your life. Picture what you would like to see. Let your mind roam free. Don't let your dreams be restricted by the reality of your current circumstances. Dare to dream of your life as you would like it to be, not necessarily as it is. Write down what you see, regardless of how frivolous or fanciful if may seem. It's your dream, your wishful thinking and the sky is the limit.

Are you the person you want to be? I know I wasn't. What and where I was at that time were not even in the same ball park as what I wanted to be.

Take a look at your dream and write down what has to change for you to make it a reality. Don't worry if the changes appear beyond the realms of possibility. We are only dreaming after all. Look at your list of changes. Mark the ones that you can effect now or in the short term, those that are within your power to make. Write down what you need to do in order to make each change. Start with yourself: you are the determining factor in your dream, the one factor you know you can change.

When you have completed the exercise, what do you have—a list of things that are not right in your life, a list of things you can change, a list of actions to make those changes? You have all of these but, more important, you have a plan, a blueprint for your life. You know where you really want to go and have some idea of what you have to do to get there. What is more, you have taken the first step to achieving your dream. You have written it down. It exists. You cannot deny it.

Realising your dream is up to you. You are the only person who can make it happen and the only person you can blame if it doesn't. Change is the key to making your dream a reality. If you do what you have always done, you will be what you have always been. Your achievements are determined by your abilities, by your desire to achieve and by the actions you take.

I found it a great benefit to share my plan with a friend, but choose carefully the friend with whom you share it. I chose the most optimistic, positive person I knew, someone who saw the disadvantages but focused on the advantages. I knew this friend would not say 'Get your feet on the ground; get your head out of the clouds; isn't it time you faced the reality of your situation?' but would say 'If that is what you want and where you want to go, I will encourage you, provide emotional support and help keep you on track'. My friend has since set her own plan in motion and we work together to achieve our goals. We also have some goals in common. We get together on a regular basis to reaffirm our plans, chart our progress and develop plans of action. At these times, we set the tasks, or short-term goals, we need to complete before our next get-together. These tasks keep us on track, working to achieve our longer-term goals. Whilst your plan is written down, it is not set in stone. As you achieve your short-term goals, you may need to adjust your medium- and long-term goals or even establish new ones.

Change will not happen simply because you want it to. You can make changes if you take some action and follow through with it. For example, I needed to make changes in my personal life, particularly in the way I related to my children. I was supposed to be the parent, the one in control, the one who set the boundaries and limits on behaviour. My children were not little monsters but I found the negotiation process frustrating and, at times, quite stressful. I was the parent, after all, although at bedtime in my house you could been forgiven for having doubts. I needed to take some positive action to change. I attended an Assertive Parenting Course. The skills and techniques I developed enabled me to make the necessary changes. Following through enabled me to maintain them.

Start by acting like the person you want to be. Fake it until you make it. If you want to be positive and assertive, act positive and assertive. Stand up straight, throw your shoulders back, look the world in the eye, talk with a firm voice and speak in full sentences. You will find that your positive physical posture will create positive emotional feedback. You will look and sound assertive. Without realising it, you will become assertive.

You are the master of your destiny. The choices you make or fail to make determine the direction and the quality of your life. You can be one of life's spectators, sitting on the sidelines, watching your life drift by, or, you can take some positive action, get into the mainstream and live your life to the full. The choice is yours.

Communicating with Government Departments

Asking questions is the display of a desire for knowledge rather than an exposure of ignorance.

I clearly recall my first visit to the Department of Social Security (DSS) to apply for the pension. I had never visited a DSS office before and had no idea what to expect. I arrived with my two children, aged 3 and 5, and took up a position at the end of the queue formed under the Pension Inquiries sign. After about 15 to 20 minutes, I reached the inquiries officer, who passed over the appropriate forms for me to complete and return. I completed the forms and again joined the queue. After another 10 to 15 minutes, which felt more like an hour, trying to entertain two children who by this stage were extremely bored, I handed in my forms and was asked to take a seat and wait to be called. Some time later my name was called and I approached the counter. I was asked to clarify some answers on the form, which I did. I was told that I would have to be interviewed before my application for the pension was accepted. This sounded reasonable. However, I was then told to come back the following day as they were too busy that day to schedule an interview. No, I could not make an appointment. I would have to come back and join the queue.

The next morning I again joined the queue, then sat and waited for my name to be called. After about 30 minutes, I was called to the counter and directed to an interview room. A young lady, about 22 years old, proceeded to ask for proof of my identity, copies of children's birth certificates and so on. Several times during the interview I came close to tears. I was an emotional wreck to start with. Having to provide information I regarded as very personal to a much younger and very impersonal lady was not an easy experience. My application for the pension was approved. I was told that I qualified for an immediate relief payment but would have to come back later in the day to collect the cheque and a letter of authorisation to cash it at a local bank.

I left that office feeling as if I had no control over my circumstances. The rules of the game had been read and laid down. The impersonal young lady had left me in no doubt as to the power of the umpire. If I had thought that my self-confidence and self-esteem were at an all-time low before my visit to the DSS, I was wrong. They hit rock bottom when I walked out of that office.

It wasn't until later that I faced the fact that, to the DSS, I was just one of thousands with the same problems. They didn't have time to nurse me and my bruised emotions through the system. The staff were as helpful and courteous as time permitted. It was up to me to make the best of the system. Learning to cope with being one of thousands, with an apparently never-ending river of paperwork, and with the waiting, was up to me.

THE FILE NUMBER MENTALITY

As a pensioner, you are assigned a number. Every time you make an inquiry or fill out a form, you need to quote that number.

If you register with the Child Support Agency, you will be assigned a case number and a pin number to access the telephone information service. You will also need to know your tax file number when making inquiries.

Your name is no longer sufficient for identification purposes. You and your circumstances have been reduced to a series of numbers. Whilst this method of identification is impersonal at best, it does identify you as an individual within the various systems.

Your self-esteem is not given a boost by having your life reduced to a series of numbers, but the numbers are there to stay, as long as you accept assistance from government departments or agencies. Learn to like your file numbers. These numbers are your key to financial, housing, medical, childcare, maintenance and other assistance.

ASKING QUESTIONS

After asking lots of questions and never really receiving the complete answer, or not asking the questions because I felt I should already know the answer or because they sounded too ridiculous, I rediscovered a basic truth: asking questions is the display of a desire for knowledge rather than an exposure of ignorance.

I had to move myself and my children from the family home into rented accommodation. I rang the DSS to determine whether I was entitled to any help in obtaining this accommodation. The question I asked was something along these lines: 'I have to move from our home. Am I entitled to any form of assistance?' The answer was 'No'. I found this difficult to understand, as I knew other people who had received assistance in the same circumstances.

Questions That Get Results

My working life had ranged from being a bank clerk, through air hostessing, secretarial work, to computer systems support and sales, I had attended many training courses and seminars and had read numerous books on the subject of eliciting information. I went to my archives and read through some of my course notes, making a list of ways to increase the effectiveness of my questions. There seemed to be six key points:

- Determine the objective of asking the question.
- Clearly define the information you require.
- Break your inquiry down into short questions (preferably open-ended questions, which cannot be answered with either 'yes' or 'no').
- If you are seeking a positive response to a question, ask a positive question.
- If the answer is negative, ask why.
- Be polite.

Armed with my list, I planned my next phone call. The objective of my call was to determine whether I was entitled to any assistance in relocating myself and my children.

What information did I need? The expenses involved would be:

- Finding the rent.
- Finding the bond.
- Having the telephone and electricity connected.
- Ongoing costs of telephone and electricity.

The questions I needed to ask, therefore, were:

- What rental assistance was I entitled to? How should I apply?
- What assistance was available to help me provide bond monies? Whom should I approach?
- What rebate or discount could I claim for initial connection and for ongoing charges from the state electricity authority? How should I go about claiming it?
- What rebate or discount was available from Telecom for connecting a telephone or for ongoing costs? What was involved in obtaining it?

Each of these questions assumed a positive response. I was assuming that I was entitled to assistance. I did not ask 'Am I entitled to...' or 'Can I get assistance with...'. As the questions were all phrased in two parts: what was available and how should I get it, 'yes' or 'no' would not suffice as answers.

I made my phone call.

The answer to the first question was that I was not entitled to receive rental assistance. Asking why, I was told that I was not entitled to rental assistance as I owned a property. I explained that, although I owned the property, I was not able to live in it, nor did I derive any financial gain such as rental income from it. I received a sympathetic hearing but rules are rules.

The answer to the next question was that I should contact Homeswest, the state housing authority, who had a scheme to aid families on low incomes to obtain private rental.

The next answer was that I was entitled to some rebate from the state electricity authority but would need to attend at their office to register as a supporting parent.

The final answer was that I would be entitled to a reduction in the connection costs and reimbursement of half the equipment rental costs each quarter. I was advised to contact Telecom.

I was polite to the inquiry officer and treated her as I would have liked to be treated, had I been in her position.

The only question that received a negative reply was the first. Using my list, I planned my next phone call to the office of my federal member of parliament. His staff listened to my problem, took details and promised to phone me back. They did, several hours later, to advise that the DSS had reversed its decision in the light of the information they had provided and I was entitled to receive rental assistance.

Obviously my planning had paid off. I now use my list to plan all my questions, whether they be by phone or by personal representation.

Inquiry officers at the various government departments are not mind readers. They will answer the questions you ask to the best of their ability and within the scope of their knowledge. Your quest for knowledge can, at times, be frustrating and it is difficult to keep your emotions in check and be objective. Remember the old adage, 'Don't shoot the messenger'. I have found that if you are polite and demonstrate a respect for their position they will, more often than not, reciprocate.

FILLING OUT FORMS

It seems, at times, that your life is regulated by the forms you are required to complete—forms applying for benefits, pension, child support or childcare fee relief, forms to maintain benefits and forms to notify changes.

The system requires a method of obtaining and updating information. So far, no one has come up with a more efficient method of doing this than with form. They probably never will.

When completing forms, there are some important things to remember:

- Read each question carefully.
- Read the instructions relating to each question carefully. If in doubt about the information required, ask for clarification.
- Answer all parts of a question—don't leave blank spaces.
- Read the questions and answers before signing, to ensure the accuracy of the information.
- Sign the form.
- Lodge the form on or before the date stipulated.

You are held accountable for all information you provide and penalties apply for incorrect or misleading information. These penalties range from possible loss of benefits to prosecution under the law. As penalties sometimes apply for late lodgement of forms, advise the organisation concerned if you are unable to meet their deadline. I have always received a fair hearing and reasonable extensions have been granted.

COPING WITH QUEUES

Waiting in line has never been one of my favourite methods of occupying time. Unfortunately, queues are a necessity when dealing with government departments and agencies. Every time you pick up the telephone to make a call to the Department of Social Security or the Child Support Agency, many others are doing just that at the same time. If you attend at the DSS or Family Court, you will find that you are not the only person who has chosen that particular time to do so. In order to deal with the inquiries on a first come, first served basis, queues are necessary. You cannot escape them.

There are some ways of minimising your waiting time, however. I have found that making a phone call to various departments at 8.30 a.m. results in no queue or a short waiting period. Similarly, arriving at the office either first thing in the morning or late in the afternoon has resulted in shorter waiting times. It requires an effort on your part to organise your time to take advantage of the lulls in traffic.

If you are attending an office in person, avoid taking young children. If this is impossible, go prepared for a wait. Take some books or a favourite toy to keep them occupied. Be sure to take a snack and a drink for the children. Be prepared for them not to behave as well as you would like. You will find that other people attending the office usually have children of their own and will be tolerant of yours.

Take something to read. If you are not watching the minutes march by, the time passes more quickly and pleasantly. Talk to the person in front of or behind you in the queue. Through these conversations, I have often discovered information I had not known about services and support facilities. Sometimes they have also provided a necessary dose of reality. You may realise that you are not as badly off as you think.

When you make telephone calls, be sure you have something to do while you wait. Read a book, write a letter, sew on buttons, do some mending or paint your fingernails. It doesn't matter what it is. How many times have you ever wished you could do two things at once? Well the opportunity is there, while you wait in the queue.

Whatever you do and however you do it, you have to find a way of coping with queues. Getting upset and frustrated will not change the fact that you will have to wait, sometimes for lengthy periods.

Housing

Change is the key to making your dream a reality. If you do what you have always done, you will be what you have always been.

There are several options when it comes to housing your family. You may be able to remain in the family home. You could seek a private rental, public housing or maybe short-term accommodation at a suitable refuge. Which option you choose depends on your circumstances.

WOMEN'S REFUGE ACCOMMODATION

Unfortunately, there are not enough refuges and their priority is to give shelter to people in danger, usually from domestic violence. But the refuges can help, so don't hesitate to call them. Many women workers at refuges have been through problems similar to those you are facing and may be able to help you find friendly, safe and supportive places to go. They can also help with legal advice and welfare housing needs. Refuge accommodation is generally short-term but can provide the respite needed to organise yourself and secure more permanent accommodation.

EMERGENCY HOUSING FOR MEN

Contact the department dealing with family and community affairs in your state. Most of them have a 24-hour or after-hours number. They will give you advice on how best to proceed. The community information pages in the front of your white pages telephone directory should also list shelters and hostel accommodation. Do not be discouraged from calling the women's refuges. They can usually provide emergency information.

REMAINING IN THE FAMILY HOME

In some circumstances, you may be able to stay in the family home with the children. In this case you may need to come to an agreement with your partner about repayment of the mortgage. The amount contributed by the non-custodial parent is usually taken into account when assessing child support payments (maintenance). These agreements are usually short-term, until the house is sold or one parent raises the finance to buy out the other.

If you remain in a home that you are buying, the Department of Social Security will not provide rental or other financial help to maintain your housing. Your state or territory housing authority may be able to provide short-term relief for meeting immediate mortgage repayments. You could also approach the bank or building society. You will generally get a sympathetic hearing from the manager, who may be prepared to suspend payments for a month or two or reduce your payments for a fixed period. The arrangement, naturally, will not be open-ended but should provide time to organise your financial position.

If you are a pensioner, you may be entitled to a concession on local and state government rates and taxes.

As custodial parent, if you remain in a rented family home with the children and assume responsibility for paying the rent, you can apply to the Department of Social Security for rent assistance.

PUBLIC HOUSING

Public (state) housing is provided by all state and territory governments. This gives many sole parent pensioners the chance to go on with their lives in a new, secure situation, at an affordable rent.

If you intend to seek public housing, act quickly. There are usually long waiting lists. The sooner you apply, the sooner you will be offered a place to live. All housing authorities have a priority list. If you are homeless or any of your children have medical problems, you may have priority.

While public housing is not free, you will be asked to pay no more than a percentage of your income (including your pension and any income you earn from working), generally between 20% and 25%, depending on the housing authority concerned.

PRIVATE RENTAL

You do, of course, have the option of renting a home in the private sector. If you have applied for public housing, you will probably have to arrange private rental while you wait for a place to become available.

Most government housing authorities can help if you have found somewhere to live but are having financial difficulties. This may take the form of providing a bond guarantee or rent assistance, if you do not qualify for such assistance from the Department of Social Security. It is important to note that any application for assistance usually needs to be made before moving into the accommodation. Your application may be denied if you have already taken up residence.

HOME PURCHASE

Should you wish to purchase your own home, most state and territory governments doprovide housing purchase loans. Repayments under these loan schemes are usually related to your income. You may be able to afford one of these loans, even if you are on a low income.

Before you decide that buying your own home is impossible, speak to your bank manager and state housing authority. At least find out what income level you would need to maintain a mortgage. If you know what income you need, you may be able to plan to afford it, if not immediately, then at some time in the future.

WHERE TO GO FOR ADVICE

The social worker at the Department of Social Security will be able to advise you about your housing options and help you find suitable accommodation. Ring your local Department of Social Security office to arrange an appointment.

Contact your state or territory housing authority (usually referred to as the Housing Department or Housing Authority) or your state or territory department dealing with community services. They will be able to advise you who to contact. Check the community information pages in the front of your telephone directory for other agencies who can help.

Child Support

You are the master of your destiny. The choices you make or fail to make determine the direction and the quality of your life. You can be one of life's spectators, sitting on the sidelines, watching your life drift by, or you can take some positive action, get into the mainstream and live your life to the full. The choice is yours.

hild support is money paid to help with the cost of keeping children, when one parent is not living with the children. It is paid to the custodial parent by the non-custodial parent.

In order to obtain the sole parent pension, you must demonstrate to the Department of Social Security that you have taken steps to get child support from the other parent.

If you have a good reason for not trying to get child support, you must talk to Social Security. This is especially important if you are afraid of violence. If Social Security agrees with your reasons, you may not have to attempt to obtain child support. Social work staff are available to help if you have problems claiming maintenance.

You can claim child support from the non-custodial parent even if you were not married and have never lived together. You can also claim child support if you are looking after someone else's children. In this case you can claim from either or both parents.

You can keep receiving child support until the child turns 18 or marries, even if you get a job or find a new partner. After the child turns 18, the court may rule that you should continue receiving maintenance if the child is still completing his or her education.

The Child Support Scheme is designed to help custodial parents and sole parent pensioners to receive child support regularly and on time.

The scheme uses the Child Support Agency (CSA) to collect payments from the non-custodial parent. Even if you go off the pension, the CSA can collect child support for you. You do not have to know where the other parent lives in order to have child support collected. The CSA is part of the Australian Taxation Office, so they can trace non-custodial parents, even if they have moved interstate.

It usually takes at least eight weeks to receive your first child support payment, if everything goes by the book. Thereafter, your child support will be paid each month, as long as the non-custodial parent pays or the CSA is able to collect it.

Non-custodial parents on very low incomes do not have to pay child support. The CSA will assess whether his or her income is high enough to pay.

The Child Support Scheme operates in two stages.

Stage 1

You come under Stage 1 if:
- Your children were all born before 1 October 1989 and
- You separated before that date (or you have never lived together).
  Under Stage 1 you must either:
- Arrange for the non-custodial parent to pay you child support privately; or
- Obtain a court order or registered agreement for child support.
  Social Security can explain this in more detail and can refer you

to legal help. If you qualify for legal aid, you will not have to pay for the lawyer.

Remember: if you have a good reason for not trying to get child support, you should talk to Social Security without delay.

Stage 2

Under Stage 2, you do not have to go to court to get child support. You come under Stage 2 if:

- You separated on or after 1 October 1989 or
- Your child/ren was/were born on or after that date.

Under Stage 2 you can either:

- Ask the CSA to set the amount and collect the payments for you; or
- Ask the CSA to work out the amount of child support you should get, then make your own arrangements to collect it from the other parent.

If you collect the payments yourself, you must get the full amount worked out by the CSA. Once you have asked the CSA to collect your child support, you cannot decide later to make your own arrangements for its collection.

If you apply to the CSA to calculate the amount for you, the child support you will get is based on a formula. This formula takes into account such things as:

- The non-custodial parent's taxable income.
- The number of children for whom you are claiming.
- The number of natural or adopted children the non-custodial parent has in his or her current family.

In calculating how much child support must be paid under Stage 2, the CSA allows the non-custodial parent a set amount for living expenses and for each natural or adopted dependent child living at their home. The custodial parent's excess income over average weekly earnings is deducted. After these deductions, a percentage of the non-custodial parent's adjusted income is paid as support for each child. The assessment is recalculated each year to allow for inflation. If the non-custodial parent is unemployed, child support is not payable.

Social Security will arrange for the child support collected by the CSA from the non-custodial parent to be paid to you.

If you were not married when the child was born, you must prove that the person from whom you are claiming child support is actually the child's parent. Documents you can use to prove this include:

• A birth certificate showing the name of that parent;
• Adoption papers; or
• A statutory declaration that he or she is the parent.

If you cannot provide any of these documents, you might have to go to court to prove the other parent's identity. Talk to Social Security if you don't have the documents.

WHAT IS COUNTED AS CHILD SUPPORT?

Child support is normally paid as regular amounts of money but it can also be in the form of:

• Payment of bills.
• Housing costs.
• School fees.
• A lump sum.

You must tell Social Security about any child support you receive.

The amount of child support you receive may affect the amount you receive in Family Payments. However, it does not affect the sole parent pension.

PRIVATE CHILD SUPPORT AGREEMENTS

If you are a pensioner, the Department of Social Security will not accept an amount paid under a private arrangement unless it is at least 90% of the child support formula. Payments must be collected by the CSA.

If you do not receive a pension, allowance or benefit and can agree with the other parent on an amount of child support, neither the CSA nor the courts need be involved. However, you can still ask the CSA to assess the amount of child support that should be paid. You can also register the agreement with the CSA, who can collect payments if you and your partner wish. If the agreement is as a result of a court order or is court-registered, it must also be registered with the CSA, regardless of whether they are to collect payment.

ENFORCEMENT OF CHILD SUPPORT ASSESSMENTS

Should the paying parent not voluntarily make payments, the CSA can have the payments deducted from any salary due. If the paying parent is self-employed or works on a commission-only basis, the CSA can apply to the courts for a summons for the amount outstanding. Where payment is still not forthcoming, they can apply for an enforcement order for confiscation of property to the value of the amount outstanding.

RIGHTS OF APPEAL

If either party feels that incorrect or misleading information was used in the assessment of child support, they can appeal to the CSA at no cost. They can also take their case to a solicitor.

If either parent's income drops by at least 15%, they can ask for a new assessment. Where a non-custodial parent's income drops by at least 15% or their current income is considerably less than at the time of assessment, that parent can request that the assessment be based on an estimate of income for the current financial year. If they underestimate their income, they will be billed by CSA when they file their tax return. Their tax refund or a proportion of it can then be taken, either as payment in full or as a contribution towards the debt. Should the income have been overestimated, payments can be reduced or suspended until the overpayment is cleared.

How To Apply For Child Support

You can obtain an application form for Child Support from your Social Security office or from the Child Support Agency in the Australian Taxation Office.

Overall, the Child Support Scheme works well in a majority of cases. If a non-custodial parent is intent on avoiding responsibility and delays payments or falsifies income details, they may cause the custodial parent unnecessary financial hardship and inconvenience. However, in order to do so, they will have to provide false or misleading information to the Taxation Department. In the end, they will have to make good the child support payments and may face penalties or prosecution by the Taxation Department.

Ways to Find That Job

If we don't strive to succeed we cannot suffer the pain of failure. If we don't put ourselves forward we cannot suffer the pain of rejection. If we don't succeed we don't have to cope with the results of success.

ost sole parents face the choice between continuing with or gaining paid employment or staying home in the role of full-time parent. It is a choice you will make depending upon your circumstances, your hopes and dreams for your future and that of your family.

Should you choose to re-enter employment, you are faced with the task of finding a suitable job. Some people are more successful in their job search than others. They were not just 'lucky' or 'in the right place at the right time'. They had at least three things in their favour:

• A positive attitude was reflected in the way they interacted with people. They were optimistic and expected to be successful, so other people responded to them favourably.

- They developed a job-prospecting system and worked at it consistently.
- Their presentation, both personal and documentary, indicated a motivated and directed person.

If job searching is not difficult enough these days, you can count on one or two more challenges in finding employment. We are now familiar with anti-discrimination and equal opportunity laws, which are designed to protect us against bias based on gender, marital status, race, religion or political affiliations. However, a prospective employer's attitudes to these is still a major factor in hiring decisions. As a sole parent, you may well have to overcome the prevailing attitude that you will be absent due to family problems, such as sick children, more often than the employee who shares those responsibilities with a partner. You may be faced with overcoming the attitude that you would be more interested in developing new relationships and enjoying your freedom than in a career.

These challenges need not discourage you. By identifying and accepting them, you will be better able to formulate a strategy for meeting them.

Whatever your approach to finding a job, it must be systematic and businesslike. Job searching is a selling exercise and, if you want to succeed, you will need to follow in the footsteps of successful marketers. You have a product, you, for which you need to find a market.

THE JOB-SEARCH CYCLE

Whether you are looking for a job after a period at home or simply trying to change the job you already have, there are several steps you need to take to make sure you end up in the right job:

- You will need to formulate a mission statement (your motivation for obtaining employment).

- You will have to spend some time brushing up on your product knowledge and decide whether your product needs further development.
- You will need to research your target market and choose your market segment.
- An effective sales presentation needs to be formulated.
- Next comes prospecting for buyers, then arranging and making sales presentations with the objective of making a sale.

Using The Job-Search Cycle

You could ignore the research, development and sales-presentation-preparation parts of this cycle and you may just strike it lucky. However, obtaining a job, the right job for you, will generally not happen by default. You will increase your chances of success with planning and consistent effort.

THE MISSION STATEMENT

What is your motivation to market your product? One of the motivators is, of course, financial gain. However, money is not the prime motivator for everyone and is generally a means to an end, rather than an end in itself. Whatever your motivation, it needs to be strong enough to sustain you through the ups and downs, highs and lows of your job search. Take the time to consider and define it. It is too important to the success of your search to be taken lightly.

PRODUCT KNOWLEDGE

How well do you know yourself? What employment-related skills do you have? If it has been some time since you were in paid employment, you may consider your skills outdated and rusty at best. If you were to substitute the words *aptitude* and *talent* for *skills* would this change your answer? What are you good at? A homemaker has skills that could apply to various occupations. As a wife and mother or father and husband, you have probably acted in at least some of these capacities:

- administrator
- advocate
- bookkeeper
- communicator
- financial controller
- fund-raiser
- manager
- marketer
- nutritionist
- organiser
- purchasing officer
- researcher
- salesperson
- teacher.

Many of the skills required to maintain a home and family are undervalued, not just in the workplace but also by homemakers.

List your skills in the order in which you would prefer to use them. At the top, place the skills you most enjoy using. Every job fits into a career type or field and involves the use of skills to perform tasks. When you decide to find a job, the first item on the agenda should be to decide in which field you would prefer to work. Do you like working with people or does manipulating information excite you? Perhaps equipment or machines appeal to you more? Let's face it, if you are a people person, working with engines will not exactly inspire or satisfy you. If you have decided to obtain paid employment, not just any job will do. It may, for a short time, but then you will be back, looking for work. One of your objectives should be to obtain employment which you will find both satisfying and financially rewarding.

Ask yourself, 'What do I most want to be? What do I most want to do?'

DETERMINING YOUR IDEAL JOB

These are some issues you may need to consider:
- Do you have any restrictions regarding geographic location?

- Do you want to work full-time, part-time, casually or be self-employed?
- What skills would you most like to use?
- To what tasks would you most like to apply those skills?
- What are your preferred working conditions?
- What financial reward would you expect?
- What arrangements would you need to make for the care of your children?

RESEARCH

Once you have a picture of your ideal job, you will need to consider how realistic your expectations are. You need to know what opportunities are available, the level of competition for that type of job and what formal qualifications will be required. Some of these avenues of inquiry might be useful:

- Make an appointment with the Jobs, Education and Training (JET) adviser at the Department of Social Security.
- Obtain a referral to the JET officer at the Commonwealth Employment Service (CES).
- Contact your nearest Commonwealth Department of Employment, Education and Training office.
- Contact the careers advice services available in your state. You will generally find a list of these in the community information section of your white pages telephone directory.
- Inquire at employment agencies, especially those specialising in placements in your chosen field.
- Speak to someone who works in your chosen field or already has your ideal job.
- Contact the union or association which represents workers in your chosen field.
- Read the classified and business sections of newspapers and trade magazines.
- Inquire at your local library.
- Seek advice from an independent career counsellor.
- Contact employers, requesting an information interview. Ask for

20 minutes of their time and stick to that time frame. Prepare questions that are likely to gain you the information you are seeking. (You can use the tips on *Framing questions that get results* from Chapter 2.)

This research will provide valuable information. It could also establish some useful contacts you can follow up when prospecting. You may find that you need to modify some components of your ideal job. You may even decide that the employment prospects within your chosen field are too limited or that the market is already over-serviced. If that is the case, it is better to find out sooner rather than later.

DEVELOPMENT

If you have carried out your research, it will indicate whether you need to undertake some 'product development'. The type of training or further education you need will depend upon your chosen field or career path.

During your research, you should have found out what level of education and expertise is required to perform your chosen job in your chosen field.

Depending on the field you have chosen, you may be able to obtain employment and study part-time. You may even find an employer who is willing to spend time and money in training you on the job. Alternatively, you may have to undertake training before seeking employment.

When considering such training, the best place to start is with the JET adviser at the Department of Social Security. He or she can arrange a referral to the JET officer at the CES. Between them, they can advise you about your options for further education. They can also inform you about benefits you may be entitled to during such education and even help with arrangements for child care. As a sole parent, you have the advantage of being able to enter CES-approved or sponsored training courses without fulfilling the waiting period applying to other unemployed people.

FINDING OUT ABOUT TRAINING OPPORTUNITIES

As in all things, various people and agencies will be able to provide information and advice but they cannot do it for you. That is up to you. Here are some suggestions for who to try:

- Some of the contacts you made while doing your research will be able to advise you about courses available and may be able to make referrals and introductions.
- You could look in the yellow pages telephone directory under 'Training' and 'Education'.
- Check the classified advertisements in newspapers and trade magazines.
- The JET adviser at CES should be able to provide a list of organisations offering training and education programs.
- There are organisations in most states assisting those who have been retrenched, need to change career paths or are considered above the optimum employment age. If the JET advisers cannot provide details of these, contact some commercial personnel placement organisations. They should be able to point you in the right direction.
- Some state governments fund schemes providing advice, referrals, counselling, personal development and training for specific groups in society. (For example, there is a scheme in Western Australia called 'Mentors for Women'.) You could enquire whether such schemes operate in your state.

If your development plan requires you to undertake further study, contact the institution (or institutions) concerned and speak to a student counsellor before enrolling. The horror stories you hear of people enrolling in wrong courses or in units which will not give themthe necessary aggregate score for completion of tertiary entrance, diploma or degree studies are numerous. It is your responsibility to obtain all the relevant information before you enrol.

If you find a relevant training course but the investment

involved is out of your reach, you could apply to the CES through the JET officer for funding. The JET officer will provide you with an application form. No application will be rejected out of hand but you can enhance your chance of approval, whatever type of work the training is for.

On the form you should state:

- The career or field in which you are seeking employment.
- Why the training will enhance your chances of obtaining employment.
- The cost and duration of training.
- A summary of your achievements, experience, skills and qualifications.

If you are applying for funding for a course that will enable you to run your own business, you will need to include details of:

- How you will deliver your services to the marketplace.
- The anticipated revenue.
- The anticipated expenses and how you plan to meet these.

If there is not enough room on the form, you could prepare a letter, resumé or business plan to accompany the application.

Applications for independent training courses will be assessed according to several criteria which include:

- The relevance of the training to your job search.
- The total cost of the training (the cost of the course plus expenses plus the value of benefits and pensions for the period).
- The competition for jobs in the career or field you have chosen.
- The number of businesses in your area providing similar products or services to yours.
- The expense involved in setting up a business in your chosen field and the likelihood of your being able to fund it.

If your application and supporting documentation demonstrate that you are motivated, directed and have done at least some homework into the viability of the training you propose, your application is more likely to succeed.

If your application is denied, be sure to ask why. You may be able to overcome the objections and have your application reassessed.

PREPARING YOUR SALES PRESENTATION

A professional, polished sales presentation is essential. Without it, you drastically reduce your chances of success. If a salesperson came to your home to sell a product, had no idea of its features and benefits and bungled the demonstration, would you be impressed?

Your product knowledge should be up to scratch by now if you have carried out the mission statement, product knowledge, research and development steps. You should know your 'features' (the skills you have to offer), and 'benefits' (what you can bring to a job).

Projecting The Right Image

Your personal presentation and grooming are of the utmost importance. You only have one chance to create a good first impression.

An employer will form opinions about your lifestyle and attitudes by the way you present yourself. Your image should reflect the standard an employer in your chosen field would expect. If you are applying for an 'up front' position with an organisation, the employer could be looking for a well-groomed, well-dressed, fashionable but understated image, which would reflect the professional image the company is trying to create. If the position is with an advertising agency projecting a professional, creative, up-to-the-minute image, you would not want to present an image of understated elegance. Your image will depend upon the type of job you are seeking. Your research should have revealed what type of image you need to create.

Creating the right image does not have to be an expensive exercise. One or two presentation outfits will do the job. If you are not particularly good at putting it together, seek advice from a friend who is. Browse through your local bookshop or library for ideas. If finance is limited (and it probably is), there are some quality bargains to be found in recycled clothing boutiques.

Perhaps you could raid the wardrobes of some friends. Many chain stores, for men and for women, have a range of inexpensive mix-and-match pieces. If you stick to one or two co-ordinating colours, you could get away with one pair of good shoes. The shoes do not have to be expensive but should be clean and unscuffed. Check the heels to ensure they are not worn down and scraped. Your handbag or briefcase should be clean and well-maintained. You may be able to borrow these from a friend if you don't have anything suitable yourself.

If clothes are an important part of your image, so is your grooming. Well-kept hair is essential. For men, ensure that your beard or moustache, if you have one, is trimmed. A trip to the hairdresser or barber may be required.

For women, your makeup should be suitable for the type of employment. Seek the advice of friends or cosmetic consultants you may know. You probably won't need a lot of new makeup but you may need to learn how to apply what you have differently. Most direct-selling cosmetic companies and some department stores offer an obligation-free facial or makeover. You might like to take advantage of this.

The accessories you choose—jewellery, belts, scarves, ties, and so on—all contribute to your image. Choose them carefully.

The image you create to obtain and maintain employment and the image you reflect in your personal life could be quite different but they serve different purposes.

Picture the visual impression you would like to make when you attend an interview. Walk to a mirror and take a look. Does the reflection you see depict that image? What! You're not dressed as you would for an interview? Why not? Job searching is a serious occupation. You are a self-employed job-seeker. You are not unemployed. The best way to avoid developing an 'unemployed consciousness' is not to consider yourself unemployed.

Many of us find it difficult to work from home. Without the office environment, procrastination can overtake us. If this is your problem, dress as if you were going off to work in your chosen field. Leave the house. If you would normally drive to work, get into your car, start the engine, turn on the radio or whatever you would normally do. Turn the engine off, get out of the car and re-enter the office to start work.

Your Sales Documents

Your personal presentation is only one part of the overall sales presentation. Your sales aids (your resumé, covering letters and other documents) also need to reflect the image you want to create.

THE RESUMÉ

The resumé serves several purposes:

- It is an overview of your experience, qualifications and achievements.
- It can form an agenda for the interview.
- It is an extended business card, something you leave behind.
- It acts as a memory jogger for the interviewer.

Resumé Pitfalls While a good resumé is essential, you can create problems for yourself by the way in which you prepare and circulate it. If it is prepared on the stationery of the company for whom you currently work or faxed on their machine, the company name and telephone number will be printed on the top of each page. Your ethics could be brought into question. A prospective employer may ask, 'How much of my time and facilities will be used for private purposes if I employ this person?' If you exaggerate (translation: lie) in your resumé and are found out, your honesty and integrity are brought into question. If you send your resumé to a prospective employer who just happens to be a friend or acquaintance of your current employer, he or she could pass an innocent comment like, 'I understand one of your employees is looking for work'. At best, your current employer will have doubts raised about your loyalty. At worst, you could get fired. If you have sent out hundreds of resumés and not had a bite, your self-esteem could take a battering.

There is no 'right' way to present a resumé. However, there are several wrong ways. You should not include in your resumé:

- Your date of birth.
- Your marital status.
- Any reference to children.
- Photographs.
- Past salaries or expected salary.
- References.

Why not? OK, let's take a look at why not.

Details of your personal life, such as whether you are married, divorced or separated, whether you have children or your age are not relevant to your qualifications for a job.

One rule of job-seeking which is written in stone is, 'Don't discuss salary until you have been offered the job'. An employer might ask for salary information for several reasons. One could be to eliminate you as a candidate. Another could be to ascertain whether you will work for less than they anticipate having to pay.

With equal opportunity laws, employers prefer to avoid being accused of turning down an applicant based on their looks. For this reason, some organisations have photographs removed from resumés before they are circulated. Unless you are applying for a job that depends upon your looks, such as modelling, it is generally not appropriate to attach one.

Unless specifically requested, written references and the names and telephone numbers of referees need not be included as part of your resumé. It is assumed that most people can provide references of some kind. If referees are requested, supply this information on a separate page, accompanying your resumé. If, however, you could gain a possible advantage by including a referee's name and telephone number, do so. This would be appropriate where the referee's name would be recognised by an employer and their opinion viewed in a favourable light.

Preparing A Good Resumé   Your resumé should be a summary of your experience and accomplishments. Avoid the temptation to 'profile' your personality. As the saying goes, 'Self-praise is no recommendation'. You are hardly going to make comment on any of your personality traits that are less than flattering.

There is some information you should always include in your resumé:

- Your name, address and telephone number should always be included. It may seem obvious to you. There are, however, some people who are still waiting for a telephone call from a prospective employer, the only problem being that they didn't include their telephone number in their resumé. It does happen. Don't let it happen to you.

- A resumé is not a resumé without details of your employment history, skills, accomplishments and volunteer experience, if relevant. Your resumé is a sales aid. It should help sell you to a prospective employer as being ideally suited for the job available. Simply providing a list of past jobs, major tasks carried out and equipment used, while informative, is just a list of features. Detailing your actual accomplishments alerts a prospective employer to the benefits you brought to a job and how your previous employer gained. If the filing system you organised, the office procedures you implemented, the financial management systems you formulated and implemented or the staff training procedures you instituted provided benefits or yielded financial gains, say so.

- Details of your education, qualifications and training should also be included. An employer will want to know what training you have had in order to carry out the job for which you are applying. Depending upon your age and work experience, you may or may not include details about high school qualifications. However, you need to ensure that any relevant certificates, training or licenses are detailed.

- If your resumé is likely to be faxed to or passed around an office, it is wise to put a heading, including your name and the page number at the top of each sheet, in case the sheets become separated from each other.

There are varying schools of thought on whether a brief summary of your qualifications should be included on the first page of your resumé. This could be an advantage when your qualifications and skills have been acquired over a period of time and several jobs or when you have a lot of relevant experience. If you lack relevant qualifications or skills, it can be wise not to include a summary as it will only draw attention to that fact. You need to weigh each side of the argument in the light of what you can offer the employer. In a busy personnel office, a lot of resumés receive only a cursory scan. After all, they receive hundreds of them. A summary will provide even the busiest scanner with a grasp of your qualifications and therefore of your suitability (or unsuitability) for consideration.

There are many books to assist you in preparing your resumé. You could also seek advice from a professional careers or placement organisation.

PROSPECTING

One method of prospecting for a job is to read the advertisements in the paper and trade magazines each day, then send off your resumé, with a letter of application, to advertisers whose jobs interest you. Well, it is one way of doing it. However, you are unlikely to hear about the large number of jobs that are not advertised.

Then there is the 'mass mail out'. You post off to organisations and companies for whom you think you may like to work your general-purpose resume with your general-purpose covering letter.

The problems with this method are:

• The letter is usually addressed to 'the Personnel Manager', 'To Whom It May Concern', 'Dear Sir or Madam', 'The Manager' or something equally impersonal.

• Your resumé does not address a specific job category.

• Your resumé does address a specific job category.

Why are these problems?

• You have not demonstrated even the most basic knowledge about the company to whom you are applying for work. You don't even know the name of the person to whom you should address your inquiry. Even employers like to feel important, that you have sought them out, that they are not just one of the crowd.

- If your resumé is too general, it may not be evident what qualities or qualifications you have, related to a specific field. Don't forget, if it is a large organisation, the person who can best evaluate your experience and skills and has the power to hire will generally not be the person who evaluates your resumé and application. If it is too hard to classify you, at best you will get 'filed away'. At worst, you will get 'binned'.

- If your resumé targets a specific job, you may well knock yourself out of contention for other jobs which you could have used as stepping stones for the job you want. As we have just seen, the person who is evaluating your application may assume that you are only interested in employment of a particular type. That person is not to know that, while you would like to be the Sales Manager or Personal Assistant to the Chief Executive Officer, you would be prepared to serve an apprenticeship as a salesperson or secretary.

While both of these approaches are useful and can be productive, they are not necessarily the only or best ways to prospect for a job.

It is a widely-held misconception that a well-presented resumé will secure a job. The resumé is a tool you use when prospecting for jobs or making your presentation at an interview. It is not the be-all and end-all of the job search.

Developing Your Network

There is a saying that it is not what you know, but who you know that makes the difference. How true this is in the job search. Use you friends and acquaintances to establish contacts in your job search. There is no substitute for face-to-face contact when looking for work.

Speak to everyone you know—your friends, family, the butcher, the baker and the candlestick-maker. Let them know that you are searching for work and your preferred field of employment. Everyone knows someone else. Take advantage of this. Network. If someone gives you the name of a person who would be a worthwhile contact, ask, 'May I use your name and say that you recommended I contact them?'. If the reply is affirmative, ask, 'Would you be willing to call them and set up an appointment for me?'.

If you are interested in working for a particular organisation, keep asking until you find someone who works there or knows an employee of that company. Ask, 'May I use your name and say that you recommended I contact them?'. If the reply is affirmative, ask, 'Would you be willing to introduce me or make an appointment for me?'. What you want is an information interview. You can find out:

- How they got their job.
- Who the personnel manager is.
- Who has the power to hire you.
- What the salary ranges are.
- What the prospects of employment with the company may be.
- Whether they have particular hiring patterns.
- Whether there are any special projects coming up for which they may require extra staff.

Everyone who works for someone is a resource in the job search.

Luck and being in the right place at the right time are a poor basis for job search. Commitment is essential. Be prepared to devote at least five hours a day, five days a week to searching. Your job is to search for work. That is how you are currently employed.

Some people make the mistake of approaching only large organisations when looking for work. Keep in mind that a lot of employment opportunities are generated by small business.

Don't underestimate the value of research. Find out as much as you can about the companies you intend to approach. You intend to generate a need for your services or to fulfil their existing needs. If you don't know what these are, how can you do this?

Always, always remember to send a thank you note to people who have assisted you in your search. Do it straight away. Don't put it off. People like to be appreciated and will continue to be co-operative and helpful as long as they feel valued. No, a thank you phone call will not do.

The Business Card

Most people in business have a card to leave behind when they go, so that people they meet will remember them. Your thank you notes can be a kind of business card.

If at all possible, however, it is worth having some cards printed or making your own. They should contain:

- Your name and address.
- Your telephone number (and fax number if you have one).
- A number where a message can be left when you are not home, if you don't have an answering machine.

You should carry some cards with you at all times. You never know when you are going to meet someone who can provide a lead or contact. Go prepared. Providing a number where a message can be left if you are not home is particularly important. You don't want to miss out on an interview because your phone kept ringing out.

Cold Prospecting

This method of prospecting involves knocking on the door and inquiring about opportunities for employment. It is more effective in some fields of endeavour than others. The company whose door you knock on may not have any vacancies but they may be able to refer you to a company which has. You could 'door knock' by telephone, using the yellow pages. This method of job searching is time-consuming and, unless you are highly motivated, can be tiresome and damaging to the self-esteem. However, it should not be rejected out of hand.

Who Makes The Hiring Decisions?

I cannot overstate the importance of meeting the person who makes the hiring decision. Organisations have various methods of screening people. Unfortunately, the person to whom this task is delegated cannot necessarily read the mind of the hirer. They usually base their selection criteria on their interpretation of the hirer's requirements. In large organisations, these people are busy and cannot devote the time required to read and evaluate all the resumés they may receive. They may only look for as long as it takes them to find a suitable number to shortlist. Your research and contacts are of the utmost importance when it comes to being noticed by the person who can hire you. Don't forget it and don't underestimate their value.

THE SALES PRESENTATION

So now you are going to the interview and need to prepare for it. Have you done any homework on the prospective employer? Do you know:

- The size of the company?
- How many employees they have?
- The name and title of the person who will conduct the interview?
- Whether that person has the power to hire you?
- Whether you would like to work for this company or these people?
- The salary range you could reasonably expect in the position?
  If the job already exists, you will also want to know:
- What does the job entail?
- Do my skills and qualifications match the job?
- How can I persuade them to hire me?
  If the job doesn't yet exist and you are hoping to create it, you will want to know:
- What needs does the organisation have?
- How can my particular mix of skills and qualifications best fulfil those needs?
- How can I persuade them to hire me?

There is no substitute for homework. You will increase your chances of being successful at the interview if you know something about the organisation and its needs. For a start, you need to establish whether you really want the job if it is offered to you.

One of the biggest mistakes that people make at an interview is to approach it with a beggar mentality. You are not begging for work. You have a unique mix of skills and experience which will benefit the employer. He or she is not doing you a favour by hiring you. If you obtain the position, it will be a mutually beneficial arrangement. OK, so there are a lot of people out there who could do the job. Only one can bring to the job what you can.

The interviewers will have a series of questions which will fall roughly into four categories:

- Why did you apply for work with their organisation?
- What can you do for them (what benefits can you bring to the position)?
- What kind of person are you?
- Can they afford you?

Their questions will be designed to ascertain whether you are:

- honest
- responsible
- capable of following rules and instructions
- a self-starter (motivated)
- able to work hard with minimum supervision
- a stable, well rounded personality
- punctual
- enthusiastic about the organisation and the prospect of working there

or:

- a complainer
- one who blames others
- lazy
- lacking motivation
- arrogant
- aggressive
- showing a tendency to slacken off
- a habitual sickie-taker.

You will have to reassure the interviewer that:

- You have the necessary skills to do the job.
- You can be relied upon to put in a full day's work.
- You have every intention of remaining in the job.
- There is no reason to expect that you would regularly be sick or absent.

- You will quickly master the job and become a productive member of the staff.
- You will fit into the organisation and be able to get on with other staff members.
- You will perform to the maximum of your capabilities.
- You will use your initiative and will not have to be over-supervised.
- You will not be lazy, irresponsible, incompetent, a gossip-monger or otherwise the cause of dissension within the organisation.
- You are more likely to bring credit than discredit to the person responsible for hiring you.

Anticipating Interview Questions

Some questions crop up regularly at interviews. It can be helpful to consider and formulate replies to some of these. They are likely to include at least some of these:

- Tell me about yourself.
- What kind of work are you looking for?
- How do you see your education and experience relating to this job?
- Don't you think you are over-qualified for this position?
- Don't you think this job is a step down for you?
- Have you done this kind of work before?
- Are you generally healthy?
- How did you get along with your co-workers at your last job?
- How often were you absent during your previous job?
- Can you tell me why there are these gaps in your work history?
- What do you consider your greatest weakness to be?
- What do you consider your greatest strengths to be?
- Where do you see yourself in five years from now?
- What are your goals in life?
- Why did you leave your last job?
- Why did your last job end?
- Why were you fired?

It is better to attend an interview having considered questions which may be asked and the replies which would be appropriate. Remember:

- Talk about yourself only if what you have to say will highlight a benefit you can bring to the job. Give the briefest of personal descriptions.
- Time your answers to last no more than a couple of minutes.
- If asked to identify a weakness, pick one that you can turn into a positive benefit.
- Ensure your answers are informative, confident and self-assured but avoid the temptation to brag.
- Avoid the temptation to make yourself look good at the expense of a previous boss or co-worker.
- Questions are asked for the purpose of eliciting information, so beware the 'harmless' question.

You could try your answers out on friends, family, associates or some of the contacts you may have made during your prospecting.

If possible, avoid any discussion of the salary level you expect until you have been offered the job. You can eliminate yourself from contention by expecting either too little or too much. If possible, get the interviewer to state the salary range they are prepared to pay and hook yours in there.

Don't forget to ask the questions for which you require answers. These will be questions that can help you determine whether you would like to work for the organisation.

Always arrive five to ten minutes early for the interview. You want to appear calm and composed, not hurried and harassed. Ensure that your appearance is flawless. It is helpful if you don't go reeking of garlic, cigarette smoke, alcohol or the like. Sit up straight. Don't slouch. Speak clearly and enunciate your words well. Don't mumble. You want to create an image of confidence and self-assurance, but don't go over the top.

After the interview, don't forget to ask, 'When can I expect to hear from you?'. Wait for the reply. If the answer is not specific, ask, 'When would be the latest I could expect to hear from you?'. Wait for the reply, then ask, 'If, for any reason, I have not heard from you by that time, may I contact you?'. Then stick to that arrangement. Apart from perhaps sending a thank you note for the opportunity of the interview, make no other contact until the agreed time.

Don't underestimate the importance of the thank you note in the right circumstances. In a situation where you are being considered with several other applicants, it may tip the scales in your favour. Be careful, however, to sum up the personality of the interviewer at the time. Some people may actually respond negatively to receiving a thank you note while they are trying to reach their decision, seeing it as 'pushy'.

If you have been for a lot of interviews but have not managed to secure employment, the chances are that something you do or do not do at the interview is letting you down. If this is the case, you could contact the interviewer. Make it clear that you are not attempting to change their mind or complaining about the fact that you were not successful. You have been considered but not selected for a number of jobs. You are sincerely interested to know whether it is something you are doing or not doing during the interview and would value their opinion. They may decline to answer or skirt around the question but they may also give you some valuable advice.

CREATING YOUR OWN JOB

One possible area of employment which people often overlook is self-employment. There are many jobs you can do, working from home. You may have talents or aptitudes that would lend themselves to this type of employment.

If you are considering working for yourself, there are several matters which must be considered. These include:

• The reasons for establishing your business.
• The aims of your business.
• The scope of your activities.
• The current status and future prospects of the industry you propose to enter.

- The advantages of your business or service over its competitors.
- The management and performance projections of your business.

You will need to do some detailed planning for your business. You should not consider starting to trade until you have developed:

- A marketing plan, showing:
  - who your competitors are
  - how you better their goods and services
  - how you will deliver your goods and services to the market.
- Financial projections for at least the next 12 months, indicating:
  - anticipated or known revenue
  - budgeted or known manufacturing and administration costs
  - cash flow forecasts, including provision for repayment of loans.
- An estimate of the amount of money you require to carry you through the initial phase of your business and a list of the uses to which this money will be put.

Now look frankly at your qualifications and experience to run this business and decide whether some extra training is required. If so, training programs are available through the CES to help you. You may need to revisit the earlier parts of this chapter.

Regardless of the type or size of business you intend to establish, the basic principles of business management should be applied.

Speak to people who are running their own businesses in the field you intend to enter. Find out from them what the advantages and disadvantages are. Ask what challenges or problems have presented themselves and how they have overcome them. Speak to the small business advisory bodies in your state to obtain information and advice. Setting up in business is not the hard part. Making it successful is. You will need to follow the same steps as you would in searching for employment:

- Write a mission statement.
- Conduct your research and product development.
- Prepare your sales presentation.
- Prospect for customers or clients.
- Make your presentation.

You will find that customers will not beat a path to your door. It will be up to you to:

- Find them.
- Establish that they have a need for your services or generate the need.
- Convince them that you are the best person to provide those services.

You will need a good financial accountant, not necessarily one who specialises in taxation.

You will find that your local council has laws governing the types of business you can run from your home and the types of advertising signs you are permitted on your property. However, the majority of businesses run from the home create little, if any, disturbance on the suburban scene and are unlikely to attract the attention of the local council.

Some businesses that can be run from home include:
- Aerobics/gym instructor
- Architect
- Artist
- Beauty therapist
- Business-related consultant (such as financial adviser)
- Cake decorator
- Caterer
- Childcare provider
- Cleaning contractor
- Desktop publisher (for brochure or newsletter preparation)
- Draftsperson
- Dressmaker
- Furniture restorer
- Graphic designer
- House- and pet-sitting contractor
- Insurance agent
- Investigator
- Ironing contractor
- Marketing consultant
- Photographer
- Potter
- Printer

- Public relations consultant
- Researcher
- Secretarial service provider
- Telemarketer
- Tradesperson (such as plumber, mechanic, electrician)
- Training consultant
- Tutor or teacher

...to mention just a few.

Your newsagent, bookshop or library will carry some publications to help your research. There are magazines which list businesses for sale. You may not want to buy one but you may find articles related to such topics as:

- Getting started in business.
- Marketing.
- Customer service.

You could also glean information about viable business opportunities, including franchises, in which the parent companies may provide a lot of support to help you get started. Contact the state government department dealing with administration of businesses and consumer affairs. They may be able to provide information and advice about a particular type of business.

DIRECT SELLING

Direct salespeople are self-employed and their financial reward is directly related to the volume of sales they make. In other words, they work for commission.

Before you get carried away with the promise of 'unlimited earning potential' or 'some of our people earn $1000 a week or more', stop and remind yourself that there is no substitute for thorough research, hard work and commitment. There are no shortcuts to success. Get-rich-quick schemes rarely work. Beware of the 'you don't have to sell the products; they sell themselves' routine or the 'you don't have to sell anything; just use it yourself and encourage friends and acquaintances to buy or sign up'. If no one is selling anything and everyone is buying at a discount price because you are all 'distributors', who is making the money? It won't be you.

There are some excellent direct-selling organisations and there are people who earn average or above-average incomes in this way. However, you need to be sure that opportunity has, in fact, knocked on your door and someone hasn't simply rung the door bell and run away. I would be particularly careful of joining organisations that put down the reputation or services provided by another organisation as part of their sales pitch.

Direct selling with the right organisation can enable you to fit your employment around the other components of your lifestyle and be rewarded in direct proportion to the effort expended. You can establish a satisfying and rewarding career. Choose carefully.

Childcare Services

Childcare services can mean the difference between sanity and insanity, prosperity and poverty, social activity and isolation. In short, they are a necessity.

hen most people think about childcare services, they tend to think in terms of having children cared for while they go to work. Of course this is a very important function of childcare services, one which the government recognises and subsidises.

However, for sole parents who are not in paid employment and are struggling to maintain some control over their lives, they can provide a much-needed respite from the demands of child-rearing. They give a breathing space, time to relax, to meet with friends or simply do nothing. As a sole parent, you don't have that break in the evenings enjoyed by two-parent families, when children's attention and demands can be shared between both their parents. There is no one to take over, to share the load. If you have no other family support structure, such as grandparents or other relatives, or friends, to step into the breach, some form of respite care is probably essential to your wellbeing. Even a few hours once a week can be heaven, particularly if the child's other parent does not have access. Just to be able to go to the shops and browse, window shop or sit and have coffee and watch the world go by, can be revitalising.

Parents who are in paid employment or are involved in full-time or part-time study still receive first priority in access to childcare. However, sole parents have priority over parents who are married (or living in a marriage-like relationship) who stay at home, with more than one child below school age. The social worker at your Department of Social Security office should be able to advise you about occasional care for your children.

WHAT SERVICES ARE AVAILABLE?

Although you may consider childcare an expensive option, many centres participate in a fee relief arrangement, funded by the Commonwealth Government. This scheme, explained later in this chapter, makes childcare much more accessible to parents on a budget. There are several types of childcare service available.

Occasional Care

These centres provide child-minding services for a few hours at a time and are sometimes run by local governments. You may be able to arrange a regular period during which you can leave your children, such as each Wednesday morning.

Day Care

These centres are operated independently. Although their primary function is to provide quality day care for parents who are working or studying, they sometimes have positions available for respite care, to enable you to relax or socialise. Not all centres participate in the fee relief scheme. It is important to ask whether they do when you inquire about placement. For information about day care:

- Contact the Commonwealth Department of Health, Housing and Community Services in your state or territory.
- Speak to the social worker or JET adviser at Social Security.
- Check the yellow pages listings under Childcare Centres or Childcare Services.

Family Day Care

As the name implies, the children are cared for at the home of a licensed operator. These people provide an alternative to the day care centre. Not all family day care operators participate in the fee relief scheme. Again, it may be possible to organise care for one or two days per week. To inquire about family day care, you could:

- Contact the Commonwealth Department of Health, Housing and Community Services in your state.
- Check the white pages listings under Family Day Care in your telephone book.
- Speak to the social worker or JET adviser at Social Security.

After-School Care

Most local governments provide an after-school care service. The children are picked up from school and taken to the after-school centre, where they are cared for until the parent finishes work. Most of these centres offer a subsidised fee scheme. Contact your local government office for more information.

Holiday Programs

Most local governments run programs during school holidays, to care for children with working parents. The after-school care centre will be able to tell you about these programs or you could contact your local government office. Fee relief is usually available for these services.

PRIORITIES IN
CHILDCARE PROVISION

The Commonwealth Childcare Services Program subsidises qualifying centres, who must use the government's guidelines to establish priority of access.

- First priority is given to parents in paid employment or undertaking some form of full-time or part-time study or training.
- Second priority is given to children or parents with a continuing disability or incapacity.
- Third priority is given to children who are or may be at risk of abuse or neglect.
- Fourth priority is given to sole parents or those at home with more than one child below school age.

   Access to these services is largely in terms of:

- The benefit of childcare to the child and the family.
- Alternative arrangements reasonably available to achieve the same benefit.
- The special needs or restricted alternatives affecting families on low incomes, sole parent families or socially-isolated families.

The amount of care provided is determined by the reason for care. Children whose parents are employed or undertaking study or training will obviously require more hours per week than those attending for respite care. As much as we would sometimes like it, full-time respite care is unlikely to be offered.

Obviously your priority of access may change with your changing circumstances. It is important to note that if you become unemployed, your priority of access is not affected while you are actively seeking employment.

CHILDCARE FEE RELIEF

This scheme, administered by the Department of Health, Housing and Community Services, can help you with childcare fees. Childcare and family day care centres approved under the Children's Services Program can offer reduced fees according to your family's income and the number of children in care. The government pays a subsidy directly to the childcare provider, then you pay less for your childcare bill. You do not have to pay the fees and apply for a refund.

The application form for childcare Fee Relief will generally answer most of your questions. However, knowing how the process works can make your application go more smoothly.

- You apply for fee relief at the Department of Social Security.
- The amount of fee relief you may receive depends upon your income and the number of children in care.
- To avoid delays in processing your application, complete as much of the form as possible and provide all the additional documentation requested.
- It may be necessary to attend an interview, either at the child care service itself or at the DSS. At the interview, a DSS officer will go through your application with you and check your proof-of-income documents. They may be able to help you obtain other documents they require. You need to present original documents but they will be returned to you.
- If you are receiving a sole parent pension or other DSS payment, they can use the income details already provided to work out your entitlement.
- Fee relief will be backdated to the day you lodge the application.
- The department will advise the childcare service of your entitlement to fee relief and they, in turn, will advise you how much you will have to pay.
- A fee relief assessment is current for six months. A new application must be completed and lodged before the current assessment expires. The childcare service should remind you four weeks before a new assessment is due.
- If you feel the assessment is incorrect, contact the fee relief assessor responsible. The assessor can explain how the assessment was made and, if necessary, re-examine your claim. Any additional information you have will be taken into consideration. Arrangements can be made for a senior officer to examine the assessment.

Supplementary Services (Sups)

If your child has special or additional needs, SUPS may be able assist with:

- Finding childcare placements.
- Providing language or interpreting services and advice to a child-care centre to help the staff provide appropriate care, if your children are from a non-English-speaking or a different cultural background.
- Helping staff meet the special needs of children with disabilities. This may mean providing special equipment and toys.
- Transport, if you have a disability and need to use childcare.

If you need more information contact the SUPS service through your nearest office of the Commonwealth Department of Health, Housing and Community services.

Using The Services Sensitively

Childcare places are limited and, at times, may be difficult to obtain. This is particularly true for respite care, due to the lower priority allocated to this type of care. However, the benefits to be gained outweigh the difficulties and frustration in obtaining it. As the saying goes, 'If at first you don't succeed, try, try, try again'. When seeking respite care, you will increase your chances of success if you make it clear that you will accept whatever placements are available. You will reduce your chances of success if you specify particular days or hours. When assessing the period of time you require childcare services for, please remember to place your child or children for the minimum period required. If those who are successful in gaining placements over-use the system, others, some in desperate need, won't get the chance to use any childcare services at all.

Managing Your Finances

Taking responsibility for your financial decisions involves facing the reality that it is always you who will ultimately face the consequences of your financial decisions. You can seek advice from family, friends or a professional financial adviser but you are the master of your financial destiny.

BUDGET PLANNING

ome people are better than others at managing their financial affairs—an obvious statement of fact. However, have you ever stopped to consider why? I know I didn't. I used the excuse that my income, no matter how carefully I managed it, wasn't sufficient to meet my commitments. It was easier to bury my head in the sand than face the reality of my situation and take responsibility for it.

Those who manage their financial affairs well are the people who have accepted personal responsibility for their circumstances and faced the reality that, ultimately, the consequences of all decisions come back to them. They have taken control of their spending habits, not let their spending habits control them.

The first step in taking such control is to establish what your spending habits are. Working with the unknown is virtually impossible. The best way to establish where your money really goes is to carry a notebook with you for up to a month and write down everything you spend. Although you may find the results, if not the exercise, depressing, you will establish a clear pattern of your spending habits and know where your money goes.

While you are carrying out the exercise for step one, you can make a start on step two. You need to establish your financial situation. To do this you will need to know the following:

Income: Your income (sources of income)
  Amounts from each source

Expenses: Cost of living (Use the budget planner in this chapter as a guide.)

  Mortgage payments
  Rent
  Food
  Car
  Childcare
  Telephone
  Electricity

Assets: Bank accounts (each bank, building society or other institution you use)

  Type of account
  Charges levied
  Interest rate
Superannuation (policy type; who with)
  Amount of payments made
  Frequency of payments

Personal insurance or life assurance (type of insurance or assurance, insurer)

    Amount paid

    Frequency of payments

Investments (type of investment)

    Amount

    Interest rate

Other assets

    Value of house

    Value of car

    Value of collections (artworks, antiques, stamps, coins, and so on.)

(Personal items, such as furniture or jewellery, are not included.)

Liabilities: Loan details (who with)

    Amount

    Interest rate

    Term remaining on loan

Credit cards (type of card)

    Amount outstanding

    Interest rate

Hire purchase (who with)

    Amount outstanding

    Term remaining on contract

Other debts (monies owing to friends, family or others).

Take a piece of paper and make the following calculation. Bear in mind that the estimated total of your living expenses may vary after you have completed the budget planner.

Total income:	$ _____
Less cost of living:	_____
Balance:	_____
Total assets:	_____
Less total liabilities:	_____
Net worth:	_____

What sort of shape are your financial affairs in? Do you have a positive or negative balance and cash flow? Is your net worth positive or negative?

If you have had to rummage around in drawers, on top of and underneath things in order to find the information required above, you have probably realised the importance of maintaining records in an orderly fashion. You don't have to set up an office, buy a filing cabinet, keep ledgers or purchase a computer but an easy-to-manage system is a must.

Buy a concertina file and label the sections according to the records you wish to keep, perhaps insurance, legal papers, certificates (such as birth or citizenship certificates), tax returns, warranties on household items, bank accounts, pension details, school fees, uniform expenses and whatever else you need. Use manila folders or envelopes for 'Accounts To Be Paid' and 'Accounts Paid And Receipts' files. Each month or each pay day, go through the 'Accounts To Be Paid' file and pay them. File them in the 'Accounts Paid And Receipts' file. When it is time to do your tax return you will have all the information at your fingertips.

Make a list of where you keep all your important documents, such as insurance and superannuation policies, your will, bank accounts, investment details and certificates, property titles and so on. You could tell a close friend or family member where this list is kept or give them a copy for safekeeping. If you become ill or travel overseas or interstate, it will then be easy for someone acting on your instructions to locate these documents, if necessary,.

Planning Your Budget

Now you are in a position to complete step three, planning your budget.

Calculate your expenses according to your pay period, whether it be weekly, fortnightly or monthly.

As there are not always four weeks in every month, you cannot simply divide by four to change a monthly expense to a weekly one. This means you must either:

• Multiply the monthly value by 12, then divide by 52.

(This brings the amount to an annual amount, then back to a weekly amount.)

Or you can:

• Divide the monthly value by 4.33.

(This is the number of weeks in a month, averaged over a whole year.)

Calculate it whichever way you find easier. Reverse the calculation to calculate monthly expenses from weekly expenses.

Allowance has been made for incidental expenses such as gifts, hairdresser or outings. These small items are easily overlooked but, as we all know, they can have a major impact on balancing a budget.

Use the following budget planner as a guide only. You may have expenses not allowed for.

Budget Planner

ITEM		ESTIMATED EXPENDITURE
TRANSPORT	*Car:* Petrol/Oil	
	Repairs/ Maintenance	
	Registration	
	Insurance	
	Driver's Licence	
	Parking/Tolls	
	Automobile Club	
	Fares	
	Taxi	
DEBTS	*Credit Cards*	
	Charge Accounts	
	Personal Loans	
	Hire Purchase	
	Family/Friends	
	Other	

ITEM		ESTIMATED EXPENDITURE
HOUSEHOLD EXPENSES	*Rent/Mortgage*	
	Rates:	
	Water	
	Council	
	Electricity/Gas	
	Telephone	
	Insurance:	
	House	
	Contents	
	Other	
	Maintenance:	
	House	
	Garden	
	Pool	
	Food:	
	Meat/Fish	
	Fruit/ Vegetables	
	General Groceries	
	Toiletries/Cleaners	
	Miscellaneous Expenses (includes such items as cigarettes and alcohol, if these are a regular part of your expenditure)	
PETS	*Food*	
	Grooming	
	Vet	
	Licensing	

ITEM		ESTIMATED EXPENDITURE
PERSONAL EXPENDITURE	*Life Assurance*	
	Medical Insurance	
	Doctor/Alternative	
	Dentist	
	Ancillary Medical (such as optometrist, podiatrist and similar services.)	
	Dry cleaning	
	Clothes	
	Hairdresser	
	Pharmaceutical	
	Entertainment	
	Magazines/papers	
	Books/Tapes etc	
	Memberships/ Subscriptions	
	Hobbies/Courses	
	Sport/Gym	
	Savings For Special Purposes (such as holidays or luxury items)	
	Other (includes such items as gambling or lotteries if these are a regular part of your expenditure)	
SAVINGS	*Personal*	
	Superannuation	
	Other	

ITEM		ESTIMATED EXPENDITURE
CHILDREN	*Babysitting*	
	Childcare	
	School fees	
	Pocket money	
	Entertainment	
	Clothes	
	Hobbies/Courses	
	Subscriptions	
	Medical	
	Life Assurance	
	Presents	
	Other	
OTHER PEOPLE	*Donations*	
	Presents	
	Other	
	TOTAL	
CALCULATING YOUR CASH FLOW	*Income Per Pay Period*	
	Costs Per Pay Period	
	BALANCE	

Now that you have established your expenses and whether your cash flow is positive or negative, you are ready to analyse your financial position.

The budget planner has been divided into various categories of expense. Check to see whether the pattern of your spending is suitable. Are you spending too much on children and other people and not enough on yourself? Are you spending too much on incidental expenses? If this is the case, perhaps some redistribution of the expenses is necessary.

If you are spending a large proportion of your income on servicing debts (credit cards, charge cards or personal loans) as a result of compulsive spending, it would be wise to seek professional advice about consolidating these debts into one loan. This would reduce your interest and charges. Although it is not wise, as a general rule, to borrow money to service debts, there are some circumstances in which it can actually save you money in the long term. However, there is no point in clearing your credit and charge cards, then simply going out on a buying binge. If this is your problem, you should also seek some counselling concerning your spending habits. If you spend every cent you earn, then resort to credit, this may be the result of a deeper problem.

Look at the pattern of your spending. Some people, when in financial difficulty, throw money away on nonessential items such as books, magazines, confectionery or knick-knacks.

You should reassess your budget at least once year or as your income alters.

It is a good idea to calculate how much of your income goes towards paying regular bills and open a bill-paying account for this purpose. When a bill comes in, you need not worry. The money is there to pay it because you have provided for it in your budget. Some budget items you could include would be:

- Telephone
- Electricity/Gas
- Car Insurance
- Car Registration
- Health Insurance
- Home Insurance
- Contents Insurance
- Life Assurance
- Subscriptions
- Rates/Water rates

Reassessing Spending Habits

Whatever the results of your budget and cash flow analysis, you need to carry out the exercise on reassessing your spending habits.

Take the notebook in which you recorded your expenditure during step one of planning your budget. Go through each day's expenditure carefully. Using the budget planner as your guide, group the expenditure into categories and note whether each was planned expenditure or impulsive. It is important to be honest with yourself.

Now look at the items, category by category. How many of the items in this list exceed your budgeted expenditure? Look at those items and check whether they were planned or impulse expenses. Do they represent essential or nonessential items (in other words, can you live without them)?

By now you should have a clear picture of where your money is going, what expenses are essential and nonessential and whether you spend more than you can really afford on impulse purchases.

Knowing your spending habits is not going to produce any miraculous results as far as your budget is concerned. In order to have a positive effect on your budget, you need to:

• Take responsibility for your financial decisions.
• Take control of your spending habits.
• Take positive action to reduce the amount of budgeted expenses, where possible.
• Seek counselling from a financial adviser, if necessary.

Let's take a look at each of these points.

Taking responsibility for your financial decisions involves facing the reality that it is always you who will ultimately face the consequence of your financial decisions. You can seek advice from family, friends or a professional financial adviser but you are the master of your financial destiny.

To take control of your spending habits, you need to face the fact that you may be an impulsive or compulsive buyer and make a sincere effort to spend only budgeted amounts on budget items. It means making decisions on what are essential or nice-to-have items in the budget.

You need to look critically at each expense and find ways to reduce it, if necessary.

For example, when you go to the supermarket, do you make a

list? Do you know what essential items you need, what luxury items you would like? Do you stroll up and down the aisles, putting into the trolley what you think you need and buying luxury items on impulse? Do you buy plain-wrapped or name-brand items? Do you buy two or three cleaning agents when, perhaps, one would do the same job? Some home-made or 'alternative' cleaning agents are just as effective as name-brand, store-bought items, but less expensive. One effective way of reducing your supermarket bill is to prepare a weekly or fort-nightly menu and shop to the menu. Instead of buying cakes and biscuits, you could cook your own. Check your pantry cupboard. What do you have stockpiled? One way to avoid stock-piling is to check the contents of cupboards and make a list before you go shopping. Keep a note pad and write down items as you run out. Shop to your list. You may already be spending within your budget but perhaps you could reduce the budgeted amount.

If you really can't seem to make your budget work despite your best efforts, you should seek advice from a professional financial adviser. This is especially important if your debt level is excessive or steadily growing. If, on the other hand, your cash flow is positive and you would like to gain maximum benefit from this by investing or, perhaps, by increasing your superannuation, a professional financial adviser may again be worth consulting.

Establishing A Financial Goal

Taking control of your financial situation and successfully budgeting to maintain a positive cash flow is an achievement. For some, the reward comes simply in the achievement itself but, for most people, the reward is in the payoff. In other words, what you get out of it. This will generally be what you want badly enough to work for it. It could be a family holiday, furniture, clothes, a house, a car, bikes for the kids, savings against a rainy day or financial security throughout your life. The list is different for each person and changes for each period of your life. However, whatever it is, you must want it badly enough.

For some people, the long-term goal is all important. For others, smaller payoffs or short- to medium-term goals are necessary along the way. Whichever category you fit into, just wanting something badly does not make it a goal. There are rules that must be followed when setting goals:

- You must write the goals down. If it's not in writing, it's a wish, a dream, and will probably never happen.
- The goals must be specific. Merely wanting to have 'more' disposable income isn't enough. Quantify the amount required. Until you do, you won't make much progress.
- The goals must be believable. If you don't believe they are achievable, you won't put in the effort.
- The goals must be vivid and exciting for you, otherwise you won't stretch to achieve them.
- You must set a time frame within which to achieve the goals.
- The goals can be adjusted. Set your goals now. They can be altered later if you set them too high or too low. Adjust them down if they become unbelievable and up if they lose their challenge.
- Review your goals regularly. Your long-term goals can only be reached by achieving your short and medium-term goals. From the achievement of these, new goals will arise.

The whole idea of setting goals is to plan your financial future, rather than muddling through and taking it as it comes. Goals allow you to take control by accepting the responsibility for making change.

Legal Assistance and Advice

It is not because things are difficult that we do not dare. It is because we do not dare that they are difficult.

Most of us have a very limited knowledge of our legal system and how it works. This type of knowledge is not high on our list of priorities until we need it. Then we need it yesterday. You should seek some form of legal advice to ensure that both your own and your children's interests are protected. If you know where to go to obtain this information, it is surprisingly easy.

FAMILY COURT

The Family Court of Australia is the best place to start. They provide a selection of brochures, pamphlets and services, covering a wide range of subjects, as well as a counselling service that will help you make decisions which will affect you and your family.

They can help you to resolve the problems which often follow the decision to separate, such as custody, guardianship, access, maintenance or property settlement. The counselling service is not restricted to people who have separated. It is available to people who intend to separate and wish to take some action to minimise the impact of the separation on their children. The pamphlet, *Marriage Breakdown and Separation*, is particularly informative. It answers the most commonly-asked questions and provides information on where to go to seek assistance.

Making an appointment with an officer of the Family Law Court counselling service should be your first step if you think you may need legal advice.

LEGAL AID
SERVICES

State governments provide a Legal Aid service, giving access to legal advice and assisting with payment of legal costs. To qualify for legal aid, your income and property must come within set limits. The means tests vary from state to state. The legal aid office in your state will be able to give you more information. If you qualify for legal aid, either a solicitor will be appointed to act on your behalf or you will receive a contribution towards your legal costs. The solicitor may be on the staff of the Legal Aid Commission or may be a private solicitor, selected from a list kept by the commission.

Legal aid is not generally granted for divorce applications or for maintenance enforcement. Aid will not normally be granted for the institution of family law proceedings unless the parties have been separated for a minimum period. However, in special circumstances, such as the need for urgent action to protect the interests of children or property, the waiting period may be waived or reduced.

The head office of each legal aid agency (telephone numbers are in the Directory of this book) will be able to give you the telephone numbers for your nearest regional office.

USING A PRIVATE LAWYER

If the Family Court counselling service can't help you resolve your problems and you do not qualify for legal aid, you will need to seek the services of a private lawyer.

Some lawyers are more experienced in family law work than others. Before you ask a lawyer to handle your affairs, ask how much family law experience he or she has. You could also speak to people who have been happy with the representation they have received and find out the name of their lawyer. A legal aid officer, a chamber magistrate at your local court or a community legal service may be able to advise you whether you need a lawyer or not.

DEPARTMENT OF SOCIAL SECURITY

You can talk to the social worker at your local Social Security office if you are having difficulties with maintenance or with a court order. While they cannot resolve your problem, they can advise you where best to seek assistance.

LEGAL COSTS

Ask your lawyer about costs at your initial consultation. He or she will be able to tell how they charge for their services and may even provide you with an estimate of the probable total cost. Some lawyers require an advance payment on account, these days, before they take on your case. Some provide a brief, free consultation initially. It can pay to shop around, especially if you live in a state where legal services are less regulated.

DISPUTING YOUR LEGAL BILL

Sometimes you can get quite a shock when you receive your account. If you think you have been charged too much, speak to your lawyer. If you are still dissatisfied with the account and the explanation and you would like to have the account reviewed, you can take it to a reviewer. You need to file a Notice Disputing Costs (Form 57), with the Registrar of the Family Court, within 28 days of receiving the account. The form can be obtained from the Registry of the Family Court. Your lawyer will be asked to file an itemised Bill of Costs and an appointment will be made for the Registrar to assess this. The process is called 'taxing the account'.

If you do not manage to complete your negotiations with the lawyer within the stipulated 28 days, you can ask for an extension of time in which to have the bill taxed. The request must be made in writing, again to the Registrar of the Family Court. It must contain an explanation of why you did not ask for the bill to be taxed within the time limit and why you believe that the account is excessive. An extension of time will only be granted if you can show that there is a good reason for the delay. You may have to attend a hearing.

There is a similar mechanism in each state for assessing lawyers' accounts relating to matters other than family law. You can request an itemised bill and ask that it be taxed by the relevant court. Be reasonably sure of your ground before you apply. It works along the following lines. If the lawyer's account proves to be justified, you will probably have to bear the costs of the assessment. If, however, the Taxing Officer reduces the lawyer's account by any substantial amount, the lawyer generally bears the costs of the assessment.

You should keep a record of the dates and durations of consultations and telephone calls. Make a note of whether you spoke to your lawyer, to the secretary or to a clerk. Keep copies of all correspondence sent to and received from your lawyer. When you receive an itemised account, you will be in a better position to judge its accuracy and whether the charges are justified. I do not intend to imply that lawyers, as a matter of course, overcharge. However, everyone can make mistakes.

Family Counselling

Your job as a parent is probably the most demanding, rewarding, frustrating and important one you will ever have in your life. Unfortunately, it is the one for which most of us are probably least prepared. The job is even harder if you are stressed out, trying to cope with your own problems, both emotional and practical. Seeking counselling is a positive and practical action, not an admission of failure.

For some reason, many people seem loath to seek counselling until their emotional problems reach crisis point. They seem to see it as an admission of ineptitude or failure as a person or parent. We need to get past our egos and accept that it is not only alright to ask for help but absurd not to. Imagine you were drowning because you couldn't swim or were disabled and someone was standing on the jetty with a rope. Would you yell out to them to throw it to you, grab it with both hands, then hang on tight while they pulled you in? Or would you think, 'Oh gosh, I can't let that person know that I really can't swim. Perhaps it would better if I drowned.' I doubt that your instinct for self-preservation would allow you to take the latter course of action unless, of course, you are a fool.

Your job as a parent is probably the most demanding, rewarding, frustrating and important one you will ever have in your life. Unfortunately, it is the one for which most of us are probably least prepared. The job is even harder if you are stressed out, trying to cope with your own problems, both emotional and practical.

The pressures on a two-parent family are difficult enough in today's social and economic climate. Those pressures are magnified in sole-parent families. Seeking counselling is a positive and practical action, not an admission of failure.

COUNSELLING
FOR THE CHILDREN

The reaction I received from friends and family when I decided to seek counselling for my daughter was mixed, to say the least. The majority opinion seemed to be that she would come to terms with the changes in her circumstances with time. I should just ride it out. Others believed that counselling would exacerbate any emotional problems she might have. Very few expected the results to be positive.

By seeking counselling for my daughter, I found that we both benefited. As she was only five, I needed to participate in her counselling sessions, providing information about the family's circumstances, the current state of my marriage, my emotional state at the time and so on. The counsellor helped me to realise that all the guilt and anger I was carting around was totally counter-productive. I really had to find some way of dealing with it. I also discovered that a child's perception of events can be very different from that of an adult, in some cases at the opposite end of the spectrum. I learned how to listen actively rather than just hear the words. I learned how to interpret my children's behaviour more accurately. I learned to respond to their behaviour rather than simply to react.

My daughter benefited from having someone neutral to talk to. She loves both her father and me. She had difficulty expressing to us how she felt because she didn't want to appear disloyal to either of us. The counsellor was someone she could trust, who wouldn't betray confidences, someone to guide her through the maze of her confusion and pain. This person could help her understand her anger and confusion and find ways of dealing with them.

Regardless of the reason for your sole parent status, the children, at any age, will experience some degree of emotional upheaval. Their lives have changed, sometimes radically, through no fault of their own. Yet we expect them to cope, when we have difficulty coping ourselves. It seems generally accepted that when the parents sort themselves out, the children will be OK. However, the behavioural and emotional problems exhibited by some children from sole-parent families gives the lie to this idea. If the children are young, obtaining counselling for them is relatively easy. As the parent, you make the decision and take the necessary action. When children are older, or teenagers, you cannot force them to attend counselling. They have to accept that they could benefit from it and see that it will have a positive result.

After speaking to many different people, from doctors, school principals, sole parents and social workers to psychologists, I have found that there are some important do's and don'ts.

- Reassure the children that any problems the family may be experiencing are not their fault.
- Reassure the children of your love and commitment to them— that although the circumstances have changed, your feelings towards them have not.
- Gently discourage false hopes and fantasies.
- Avoid using the children as an instrument of revenge. They are innocent parties and should not be made to suffer unnecessarily for a conflict between their parents.
- Avoid unloading your emotional baggage onto your children.
- Parents should avoid putting each other down in front of

children. They love both parents and it is painful and confusing for them.

- Avoid using children as messengers or intelligence-gatherers.
- Make an effort to ensure that the handovers for access are calm. If necessary, arrange for the children to be collected and returned at the home of a third party.
- Notify the school of the change in circumstances. Make an appointment to see the class teacher or principal or both. If they are aware of the situation, they can take some positive action to deal with any learning or behavioural problems that may arise.
- Let children know that it is OK to be angry with mum or dad and help them to find creative ways to let that anger out.
- Listen to them.
- Don't over-compensate.

COUNSELLING FOR THE PARENT

We often find it easier to put up our hands and ask for help for others than for ourselves. If it is worthwhile seeking help for our children to cope, why not for ourselves? A parting in any relationship, whatever the cause, usually results in varying degrees of stress or depression. Not only do you have to put yourself back together emotionally, you also have to cope with the practicalities of life at a time when you are probably least equipped to do so. If you are fortunate, you will have a network of friends and family you can call on for emotional and practical support. If not, the feelings of loneliness and isolation are magnified.

Regardless of your support network, it is helpful to have an impartial person with whom you can discuss your emotional and practical problems. Although friends and family mean well, their efforts to be understanding and sympathetic can result in justifying your negative emotions and feeding your self-pity. It is an unfortunate fact that negative emotions feed upon themselves and create dependencies.

You may find, as I did, that coping with the practicalities of life left little time for coping with emotional problems. It was easier and sometimes less painful to push them aside, rather than to acknowledge and deal with them. As a result, the see-saw that was my life was so out of balance that the negative end was firmly on the ground and the positives weighed too little to bring it back into balance. I was immobilised. I finally realised that asking for help, however difficult it may be, was the only rational thing to do.

RESOLVING CONFLICT

Conflicts within families are often difficult to resolve. Two or more people may be so vigorously defending their positions that the reason for the conflict is not defined and is blown out of all proportion. We tend to think of conflict resolution as getting our own way or being proved right. Why choose being right instead of being happy, when we know there is no way any of us can be right all the time?

Most people react negatively in a family conflict, perhaps because we become anxious and attempt to resolve it from a negative perspective. Conflict can place enormous strain on a relationship. If not dealt with effectively, it can cause permanent damage.

The resolution of any conflict involves negotiation. Even the cessation of war involves peace negotiations. Each person involved in the negotiations has to come away feeling as though they have achieved a satisfactory result.

In sport, referees are present to ensure each team gets a fair go. Seeking assistance in a family conflict from a 'referee' can often resolve what may, at first, appear to be unresolvable. The referee can ensure that each person is, at least, heard. They can encourage the parties to listen to what is actually being said, rather than assume what is going to be said. Quite often it is what is not heard or is left unsaid that compounds the conflict.

WHERE TO GO
FOR COUNSELLING

There are many sources of help in the community for dealing with conflicts or emotional disturbances in your family.

- You can speak to your family doctor, who can make the necessary referrals for professional counselling.
- The social worker at your Department of Social Security office is well qualified to assist you and to make referrals.
- Your state government departments dealing with health and with community matters usually provide counselling services.
- The Family Court Counselling Service will be able to help and can provide information about other available services. They also have some booklets answering questions which children often ask concerning separation and divorce. Their booklet entitled, *Children and Separation*, contains particularly valuable information.
- Your state government may have a Women's Advisory Council or Women's Information Service.
- You can contact lone-parent support groups, who may be able to offer advice and information.
- Grief counselling services, which can be located in the white pages of the telephone book, provide counselling and support after the death of a partner.
- *Outcare* is an organisation providing support to families when a partner is in gaol.

Parent Support Groups

You did not reach the enviable state of sole parenthood without help. Neither do you have to cope with it alone. Many have gone before you and many more will follow.

t is often not possible to continue with the social life you had established prior to becoming a sole parent. A majority of your friends may be couples and you might feel the odd one out at social gatherings. If you have not made an attempt to keep up with old friends, you may find that most of your friends were introduced to you by your partner. Perhaps you might feel that you cannot or should not continue those friendships. Your self-esteem and confidence could be at a subterranean level. You may even feel that you have nothing of value to offer in a social situation, nor do you have the confidence to try. Perhaps you are focussing on your children, trying to fill the gap that lack of a partner has opened in your life. They may feel like the one constant in your life, when everything else seems to be falling apart. The reasons are many and varied and may be quite complex.

Apart from the emotional reasons, there are also practical reasons why socialising is difficult. Perhaps you don't have friends or family who could babysit for you and you cannot afford to pay upwards of $7.00 an hour to a service. The 'singles' scene could be a puzzle to you. For people who are alone after a long-term relationship or marriage, the 'single' scene could be compared with being an intergalactic traveller, arriving on a planet where all the rules have changed, the inhabitants speak a different language, and etiquette and protocol are a mystery.

Sole parent support groups are a way of establishing social interaction with a group of people, all of whom are the odd one out, in a friendly and supportive atmosphere. Apart from the obvious benefit of overcoming the 'socialisation syndrome', you gain access to a wealth of advice and information from people who have gone before you. These are people who understand all that you are going through because they, themselves, have been there. You will find they can be empathetic without being judgmental or reinforcing the negatives in your life. They can be encouraging and provide practical advice and assistance in your quest to take control of and redirect your life. However, it is up to you to make the first contact. They will not seek you out.

Whilst these organisations are not generally staffed with 'professionals', they can certainly provide information and referrals for those who require it.

Many people actively involved or simply participating in sole parent support groups maintain that the friendships they and their children have developed have been a key factor in the reconstruction of their lives. Most joined to help themselves and by doing so are helping each other.

The range of activities offered by these groups varies from family picnics to day and evening social functions. They range from coffee and lunch through dinner, dancing and outings to the movies. They may offer special-interest guest speakers from such organisations as the Family Court or the Child Support Agency.

It would seem that support groups with names like Sole Parents of Australia, Parents Without Partners or Single Parents of Australia suffer an image problem. They may be perceived to be 'meat markets', where one goes when one is desperate to form a relationship. As with all organisations, you will find a wide range of personallity types. Some people will join these organisations with a view to forming a new relationship, whether it be for the long or the short term. However, the overwhelming majority do so to provide social interaction for themselves and their families, in a friendly, supportive atmosphere.

The names of support groups vary from state to state, as do the type of activities they offer. You will generally find them listed in the white pages telephone directory, under Parents, Single or Sole. They may also appear in the yellow pages, under Organisations, or in the Parent Support Services directories available from the governments of Western Australia and New South Wales. The DSS social worker (or sometimes your church or religious group) should also be able to provide you with information. Some numbers are in the telephone list at the back of this book.

All You Need to Know About the Department of Social Security

A door which you may previously have considered closed, is now being held open for you. It is up to you whether you take advantage of the opportunity and walk through the door. If you elect to remain where you are, be honest enough with yourself to admit that it is your choice. Other sole parents have faced the same obstacles which you perceive will hold you back but they have moved forward.

What is the Department of Social Security and what services do they provide? Many of us who have previously had little or no exposure to the department really don't know the answer. The best way of describing the Department of Social Security is to quote from its 'Information Handbook' of 1992.

The social security system in Australia forms a vital part of the government's social justice strategy. It provides income support to people and families who are without an adequate income for reasons such as age, disability, unemployment or sole parenthood. It also provides the framework to support access to employment for those with the ability to participate in the work force.

The charter of this body is

to deliver social security entitlements with fairness, courtesy and efficiency.

PROGRAMS

Social Security programs providing payments are numerous, covering all aspects of life.

Programs For Families With Children:
- Basic Family Payment.
- Additional Family Payment.
- Child Disability Allowance.
- Multiple Birth Payment.
- Double Orphan Pension.
- Sole Parent Pension.
- Jobs, Education and Training (JET).
- Child Support Scheme.
- A limited role in the administration of Childcare Assistance Relief.

Programs For The Unemployed Or Sick:
- Job Search Allowance.
- Newstart Allowance.

- Sickness Allowance.
- Young Homeless Allowance.

Programs Relating To Disabilities:
- Disability Support Pension.
- Carer Pension.
- Mobility Allowance.
- Wife Pension.

Programs For The Retired:
- Age Pension.
- Wife Pension.
- Pharmaceutical Allowance.

Programs For People In Special Circumstances:
- Special Benefit.
- Widowed Person Allowance.
- Widow Pension Class B.
- Guardian Allowance.
- Training Allowance.
- Rent Assistance.
- Remote Area Allowance.
- Bereavement Allowance.

All these programs can seem quite a maze at first glance. In this chapter, we shall take a look at the programs which might relate to you as a sole parent and how they operate.

LEGAL BASIS FOR PAYMENT

Social Security payments are regulated by Federal Government Acts of Parliament. Authority for paying pensions, allowances or benefits is contained in the Social Security Act, 1991.

The Act contains precise and specific conditions about qualifications for payment, the amount and the calculation of payment and the conditions governing continued payment. Actual figures have not been quoted here as they are regularly reviewed in the light of economic conditions. (You may also find details of some programs altered due to legislative or policy changes since the publication of this book.)

STRUCTURE OF THE DEPARTMENT

Social Security's organisational structure consists of:
- A client service network of regional and local offices.
- Area offices, which provide management support to a group of regional offices and give specialised services to outside organisations and individuals.
- A National Administration, located in Canberra, to oversee management and policy development.

Regional Offices

Regional offices are located in a large number of urban and rural centres. Here, the majority of social security programs are administered and the daily contact with the public occurs. These offices are open Monday to Friday. They all close for half a day per week.

Your local regional office is your key contact for inquiries about the range of social security payments and services. A list of locations of regional offices is provided at the end of this chapter, including those where Aboriginal and Torres Strait Liaison Officers or interpreting services are available. You can contact regional offices in a variety of ways.

CONTACT BY TELEPHONE

You can call all regional offices on a special number (132468), for the cost of a local call. If you live in an area remote from your nearest office, you can reverse the charges on telephone calls to that office or you can make an STD call to the office and ask an officer to return the call.

PERSONAL CONTACT

It is not necessary to make an appointment before you visit an office but if you do, you will be sure that the appropriate officer is available. Your initial contact will be with a counter assessor, who can answer general inquiries and refer more specific ones to the appropriate officer or social worker.

HOME VISITS

A Social Security Officer may visit you at home if:

- You have difficulty in getting to a regional office because of illness, transport problems or physical difficulties;
- You prefer to see a social worker or welfare officer in the privacy and comfort of your home; or
- A review of your claim is required.

All Social Security Officers who visit people in their homes have a personal Social Security identity card with a photograph. Officers should produce the card and introduce themsleves. If you doubt their identity, check with the nearest regional office before you answer any questions or allow access to your home.

Advisory Services

Many regional offices provide a regular visiting service to major outlying country centres in the region. On these visits, Social Security Officers provide payment information, conduct interviews, receive claims and review forms. The location and times of country visits are advertised in the local press and can be obtained by telephoning your regional office.

The regional office can also provide:

- Social work services.
- Services for migrants (such as interpreters).
- Services for Aboriginals and Torres Strait Islanders (such as Aboriginal and Torres Strait liaison officers).
- A financial information service (FIS).
- Services for people with disabilities (such as Disability Support Officers).

- Advisors on jobs, education and training (JET).
- Information in the form of leaflets, posters and so on.
- Speakers for seminars.
- Consultation with other departments and organisations.

THE SOLE PARENT PENSION

A sole parent is defined by the department as:
- A person who is not a member of a couple;
- A member of a couple who is living separately and apart from their partner;
- A person whose partner or de facto partner has been imprisoned for at least 14 days;
- A person left caring for a child and unable to live with their partner in the matrimonial home, because of the partner's illness or infirmity, which is likely to continue indefinitely and prevents the partner from caring for the child;
- A person whose de facto partner has died;
- A widow or widower; or
- A divorced person.

The purpose of the sole parent pension is 'to provide assistance to sole parents who are supporting at least one child under 16'.

Who Is Eligible For A Sole Parent Pension?

To qualify for a sole parent pension, a person must:
- Not be a member of a couple, or be living apart from their partner, and
- Have legal custody of at least one qualifying dependent child or have the long-term care and control of a child for at least 12 months and be likely to retain care and control permanently or indefinitely, and
- Not be in receipt of another social security pension, Veterans' Affairs service or War Widow's pension, and
- Take reasonable steps to obtain child support (maintenance) payments from a former partner/parent of their child(ren).

There is no period of prior residence required if the person becomes a sole parent in Australia.

How To Apply For The Pension

You will need to go to the Department of Social Security Office in your area, complete an application form and undergo an interview. The interview will be carried out in private by a member of the DSS staff. You may be upset and stressed by the circumstances leading up to your making the application. However, even if it doesn't seem like it at the time, you will be dealt with as expeditiously and considerately as possible.

You will need to take documents proving your identity. At least three documents from separate sources may be needed to confirm the name you use in daily living, your current address and your marital status, if applicable.

Photocopies are not acceptable unless accompanied by the original documents.

Examples of acceptable documents include:

- An Australian passport or Certificate of Australian Citizenship.
- A current overseas passport, stamped for entry to Australia.
- An Australian birth certificate or extract issued at least 12 months ago.
- Citizenship papers.
- A Proof Of Identity document from the Department of Foreign Affairs.
- Real estate title deed or mortgage papers.
- School reports, examination certificates.
- A driver's licence showing the same address as on your claim.
- Motoring organisation membership papers more than 12 months old, with the same address as on your claim.
- Paid motor vehicle registration papers with the same address as on your claim.
- A letter from a government department with the same address as on your claim.

- An employer's reference.
- A gas, electricity or telephone account in your name, showing it was paid for your current address.
- Legal documents, such as summonses, bail papers or traffic infringement notices (with motor vehicle registration papers).
- Bank, credit union or building society books more than 12 months old.
- Insurance renewal papers with the same name and address as on your claim.
- A tax assessment notice.
- An Australian marriage certificate issued by a government department.
- Rates notices with your current address.
- Divorce papers.
- A child's or partner's death certificate issued more than 12 months ago, with your name on it.
- A medical contribution book over 12 months old.

If you feel that you may be unable to produce the required number of acceptable documents to prove who you are, you could call the Department of Social Security TeleService, on their special number (132468), or ask the counter staff for help.

You will also need to provide details of your current financial situation and proof of amounts held in any bank, credit union or building society accounts. Details of your assets will be required. It is important to note that the value of assets which may be held before they affect the pension is quite generous.

ASSESSABLE ASSETS

Assessable assets include:
- Cash and money in bank, building society or credit union accounts (including interest-free accounts); interest-bearing deposits; fixed deposits; bonds; debentures; shares; property trusts; friendly society bonds and other managed investments.
- Value of real estate, (includes holiday homes).
- Value of businesses and farms, including goodwill.

- Surrender value of life insurance policies.
- Amounts disposed of without adequate financial return.
- Value of gifts above certain amounts.
- Value of loans (including interest-free loans) to family trusts, members of the family, organisations and so on.
- Motor vehicles, boats and caravans not used as homes.
- Household contents and personal effects.
- Collections for trading, investment or hobby purposes.

EXEMPT ASSETS

Exempt assets (those disregarded in pension, allowance and benefit assessment) include:
- Principal home and surrounding land not exceeding 2 hectares.
- Life interest (not created by the pensioner or beneficiary).
- Victorian Ministry for Housing — moveable unit.
- Reversionary, remainder and contingent interest (not created by the person receiving a pension, allowance or benefit).
- Interest in an estate (not received or not able to be received).
- Medal or decoration for valour (not held for investment or hobby purposes).
- Amount paid in advance for funeral expenses or a cemetery plot.
- Aids for disabled people.
- Gift cars provided by Department of Veterans' Affairs.
- The proceeds from the sale of previous home which will be applied within 12 months to the purchase of another home.
- Compulsorily-preserved superannuation if the person claiming is below age-pension age and the monies are not accessed.

(Some of these terms are rather legalistic and you may not be sure what they mean. If you are not sure whether some of these categories apply to you, the staff at the DSS office will be happy to advise you.)

Documentary evidence of your children and of their ages will be required. Birth certificates are usually enough. If you are receiving the basic family payment, the birth certificates attached to your family payment application will be sufficient.

YOUR INTERVIEW

During the interview, you will be asked questions relating to the answers you have provided on your application. You may be required to provide further information. Personal questions about your relationships may be asked. The interviewer should tell you why the information is needed, the legal authority for the request and what circumstances could result in that information being passed to another person, department or authority.

When you receive a pension, you automatically receive basic and additional family payments plus a guardian allowance. The interviewer will explain how your entitlements will be paid. You will be asked to nominate an account into which they can be deposited each fortnight.

Ask the interviewer any questions you may have about your entitlements. If possible, ask for an appointment to see the social worker as well. The interviewer's responsibility is only to check the the information you have provided, to determine your eligibility for the sole parent pension and associated benefits and to see whether your income or child support payments affect these. The social worker, on the other hand, can advise you about problems to do with finance, housing or children and can refer you to organisations offering practical or emotional support.

You will be notified in writing of the result of your application. This letter will tell you the amount of your pension and other benefits, when payments will be made and how the amounts were calculated. It will also tell you the assessed value of your assets and the value of assets you may hold, before you must notify the DSS. Printed on the back of the letter is information about notifiable events, income, assets, reviews, changes of address and your rights. Read this letter carefully. Should you have any queries or disagree with the way in which your entitlements have been calculated, contact the DSS on the number provided. It is a good idea to file correspondence received from the Department of Social Security. You will need to refer to it from time to time. You will also need to have correspondence available when making inquiries.

Pensioner Health Benefits Card

The pensioner health benefits card and transport concession card are issued when a pension is granted. They are renewed at the beginning of each year.

Concessions vary from state to state. If you are travelling to another state you will need to check whether a particular concession is available. Concessions to which you may be entitled include:

- Free or subsidised services from your:
  - doctor
  - pathologist
  - radiologist
  - dentist
  - ambulance service
  - optometrist.
- Subsidy on the cost of:
  - spectacles
  - hearing aids (from Australian Hearing Services)
  - pharmaceutical items on National Health prescriptions.
- Travel and transport assistance, including:
  - travel costs for specialist treatment, if you live more than 50km from the metropolitan area
  - concession travel on rail and bus services
  - reduced motor driver's licence renewal fee.
- Subsidies on household services, such as:
  - Supply Charge Rebate, Dependent Child Rebate and Accounts Establishment Fee Exemption from your Electricity and Gas providers
  - reduction in council and government rates and charges
  - telephone connection fee concessions
  - assistance with clothing and amenities charges for secondary school children
  - financial assistance for students aged 16 or over through Austudy.

In addition, state housing authorities have a number of options to ensure low income earners have access to affordable housing. An information leaflet detailing the concessions available in your state is available from the Department of Social Security.

Education Payments

Sole parent pensioners studying Austudy-approved courses, either full-time or part-time, are eligible for a fortnightly Austudy Supplement. You need to apply to the Commonwealth Department of Employment, Education and Training. Once you have qualified for this supplement, you should present the notification to Social Security.

If you are beginning or continuing a course and are eligible for the Austudy supplement, you are also eligible for an annual education entry payment.

Employment Payments

An employment entry payment is paid to sole parent pensioners whose earnings rise above a threshold amount. This amount changes three times a year, according to the CPI.

Jobs Education and Training (JET)

JET is a program to help sole parent pensioners back into the workforce. It is part of the government's social justice objectives to assist people to have equal opportunities and to achieve economic independence.

The service comprises integrated assistance from three departments:

• Department of Social Security (DSS).
• Department of Employment, Education and Training (DEET) .
• Department of Health, Housing and Community Services (DHH&CS).

JET provides vocational advice, training, education, job search assistance and childcare support. Participation is voluntary and is open to all sole parent pensioners. However, three particular groups of sole parent pensioners are invited to take part in the program. These are:

- Sole parent pensioners with school-aged children.
- Those whose youngest child will turn 16 within two years.
- Teenage sole parent pensioners.

KEY FEATURES OF THE PROGRAM

JET advisers from the Department of Social Security help sole parent pensioners to identify their individual barriers to employment and develop a plan of action. They give information and advice about a range of services available (including education, employment and training programs and childcare) and provide a linkage to these services.

JET Contact Officers in CES offices help to find jobs and places in training courses.

Where permanent places are available, the Department of Health, Housing and Community Services can arrange additional temporary childcare places, through the Services for Families with Children Program. These are for JET clients who:

- Are participating in a course;
- Are within a four-week job-search period; or
- Are within the first 16 weeks of their employment.

Where appropriate, referral is arranged to other welfare agencies for services not provided by DSS, DEET or DHH&CS.

Even if you do not fall into one of the three categories of sole parents specified in the JET scheme, you may ask to be included in the scheme. The training courses and counselling available to JET candidates, from day one as a sole parent, are not available to other people until they have been unemployed for 6 to 12 months or more. You are being provided with a special opportunity to achieve economic and social independence. The door to further your education, which you may previously have considered closed, is now being held open for you. It is up to you whether you take advantage of the opportunity and walk through the door. If you elect to remain where you are, be honest enough with yourself to admit that it is your choice. Other sole parents have faced the same obstacles, which you perceive will hold you back, but they have moved forward.

Guardian Allowance

Guardian allowance is a payment made to sole parents with dependent children, in recognition of the extra costs faced by parents raising children on their own. It is paid at one rate regardless of how many children a person has.

As a sole parent, if you are eligible for additional family payment, you will also be eligible to receive guardian allowance as part of the additional family payment if:

- You satisfy the means test;
- You are a pensioner/allowee/beneficiary; or
- You are separated from your spouse because of illness and have the care of a child.

Rent Assistance

If you pay government rent, own your own home or are in the process of paying off a mortgage, you are not entitled to rent assistance. (Government rent is already subsidised.)

There is a minimum weekly rental which has to be paid before your family can qualify for rent assistance. Rent assistance is paid at a percentage of every dollar of rent over that amount, up to a set maximum. The precise amounts vary from time to time as economic circumstances change.

If you are paying board and lodging, you will be asked to identify the portion of your payment which is for lodging. This amount is counted as rent. If you are unable to specify a figure, two-thirds of the board and lodging payments will be counted as rent.

When applying for rent assistance, you will need to provide proof of the amount of rent paid. A receipt will usually do. You will also need to provide details about your landlord.

FAMILY PAYMENT

The family payment is a tax-free allowance, paid to help parents with the cost of raising their children. From 1 January 1993 a sole, integrated family payment replaced the family allowance and family allowance supplement.

The new family payment has a two-tier structure:
- The basic rate, equivalent to what was family allowance.
- The additional amount, which was called the Family Allowance Supplement or Additional Pension Allowance, the Guardian Allowance and Rent Assistance.

The assets test does not generally apply to families who qualify for family payment. In nearly all cases, these clients have already met a more stringent assets test to qualify for their other income support payments. These families will receive both basic and additional family payment, free of income and assets testing.

Children Over 16 years

Family payment is only payable for dependent children over 16 if they are full-time students and have not qualified for a prescribed education scheme payment, such as:
- Austudy;
- Abstudy;
- A Veteran's Children Education Scheme payment; or
- A Commonwealth Postgraduate Awards Scheme payment.

In these cases, family payment will be extended to the end of the calendar year in which a student turns 18, or to the end of secondary schooling, whichever comes first.

Lump Sum Advance of Family Payment

From 1 January 1993, families can be paid part of their family payment in a lump sum, before it is normally due. The rest of your family payment will continue to be paid fortnightly.

You can obtain a lump sum in advance every six months. You may ask for it to be paid every six months, in January and July, with one request. When you no longer want it, tell the DSS and full fortnightly payments will start again in the following January or July.

You can ask for it just once or each time you want it. The lump sum advance will go to the account into which your family payment is paid. The amount you will receive is determined by when you make the request. For example, if you ask for the lump sum in March, it will be paid for three months (from the end of March to the end of June).

MAINTENANCE ACTION AND THE MAINTENANCE INCOME TEST

If you have children from a previous relationship, you will be required to take action to obtain child support (maintenance) for those children, if possible. If you do not, additional family payment will not be paid for the child or children concerned, although basic family payment will continue to be paid.

Any maintenance you receive will be taken into account in calculating your additional family payment, including rent assistance and guardian allowance, if applicable. The basic family payment will not be affected.

Maintenance Free Area

The maintenance free area refers to the amount of child support you are allowed before your pension starts to be reduced. This amount is indexed each July.

INCOME AND THE PENSION

Any income which you earn may affect your sole parent pension. Regular pension payments enable many sole parent pensioners to care for their children and get on with their lives. The pension enables them to extricate themselves and their children from domestic violence situations or unhappy marriages or to survive when abandoned.

For these people, their reliance on the pension is emotional as well as practical. The thought of losing this regular income, however limited, is frightening. If you have been in this situation, getting a job and re-entering the workforce, if it means losing the pension and its entitlements, is not an option easily taken up.

It is therefore important to note that obtaining paid work does not necessarily mean the loss of your pension. By the time it does, you would be earning twice what the pension itself is worth. If you stop working, you can apply for resumption of the pension.

The Income Free Area

The income free area refers to the amount of extra income you can earn before your pension starts to be reduced. This amount is a flat $44, plus $12 per child; this is how much you can earn per week before your pension is affected. For every $1 you earn over this income free area, your pension is reduced by 50c. If you have any earnings credit (see below), your pension will not start to be reduced until this amount has been used, even if you earn more than your income free area.

The basic income free area is indexed every July.

Earnings Credit

An earnings credit is a way of saving up any income free area amounts you do not use. The amount saved can then be credited against earned income. This means that any money you get from a job will not reduce your pension until the earnings credit amount you have saved is reached. For example:

- Janet, a sole parent pensioner with three children, has an income free area of $80 a week. This amount was calculated like this: $44 + $36 ($12 x 3). When Janet first starts getting the pension she is not earning any extra money.
- After 12 weeks on the pension, Janet finds a casual job. Because she has not earned any extra income for 12 weeks she has saved an earnings credit of $960.
- When she first starts work, she will receive her full pension plus her full wage.
- Her pension only starts to be reduced when she has earned wages equal to her earnings credit of $960.
- If she stops working, Janet can again save up an earnings credit amount to use if she gets more work.

Note: An earnings credit can only be used against income received from a job. Like many other benefits, the earnings credit limit is indexed in July.

CHILD DISABILITY
ALLOWANCE (CDA)

If you have disabled children to care for at home, you can apply for this allowance. You will qualify for it if:
• The disabled child is your dependant; and
• You or your partner provide the child with additional care and attention on a daily basis because of the disability; and
• You live in the same house as the child.
If your child is eligible for a disability allowance, the family payment income and assets tests do not apply.

In the eyes of the DSS, a disabled child is defined as one who:
• Has a physical, intellectual or psychiatric disability.
• Needs substantially more daily care and attention, because of that disability, than is needed by a non-disabled child of the same age.
• Is likely to need that care and attention permanently or for an extended period.

Entitlement to child disability allowance is decided on the amount of extra care and attention needed and not on the type of disability, nor on the financial costs involved.

The child must be under 16 years old or a full-time student under 25 years old, as long as they are wholly or substantially dependent on you (if you are the claimant). The child or student must not receive a social security income support payment in his or her own right but, as carer, you can certainly earn an income, as there is no income or assets test for this allowance.

How To Claim

Child disability allowance claim forms are available at any Social Security office. Part of the form is completed by you and part by the doctor who supervises the child's treatment.

You also need to provide evidence from other professionals, such as speech therapists or psychologists, who are involved in the child's treatment or can vouch for the special care and attention the child needs, because of the disability.

The opinion of a Commonwealth Medical Officer (CMO) is usually obtained to help Social Security decide whether you qualify for a child disability allowance. The CMOs only provide opinions. They do not make a decision regarding entitlement.

In some instances, a Social Security social worker may make a home visit, to gather more details, to assess the claim and to offer information on support services available.

Payment Information

If you claim a child disability allowance within 12 months of qualifying, you are entitled to back-payment from the next payday after you actually qualified. This might be the case where, for example, your child suffered an accident and you were not aware until later that you could claim the allowance. In this case, the allowance will be paid back to the payday after the date when the child began to need the extra care.

If you lodge a claim more than 12 months after the date of qualifying, you cannot claim more than 12 months arrears of child disability allowance. The allowance may be paid for this period, provided no other factor affects payment during that time.

Reviews Of Your
Child Disability Allowance

Your entitlements will be reviewed at regular intervals, along with your other pension and benefit reviews and whenever your circumstances change. This might be, for example, when the child leaves your care and control, returns to full-time education or turns 16. Medical reviews may also be conducted at regular intervals to ensure that the care and attention test is still satisfied.

Medical Examination

At any time during the assessment of a claim or during payment, the disabled child may be required to undergo a medical examination by a specified doctor. These examinations will be conducted when the child's medical condition may have changed.

Where you need to bring the child to the city or to a regional town for a medical examination, the cost may be met by the department. There is no reimbursement if the journey is within the area in which you would normally travel for other purposes, such as shopping.

Absences Of The Child From The Family Home

Child disability allowance can continue while your child is temporarily absent from your family home. If the child is away receiving respite care, you can continue receiving child disability allowance for periods of up to a total of 42 days within a calendar year, or longer in special circumstances. These respite provisions are quite separate from regular absences of the child from home to receive education, training or treatment. Such absences are not regarded as temporary. At these times, your child disability allowance will only be paid for the days the child actually spends at home.

TAXATION AND SOCIAL SECURITY

Just like other forms of income, pensions and benefits are liable to taxation but you may also qualify for rebates.

Tax Relief

Once you have found a job, you will be able to claim tax relief in the form of the sole parent rebate. A rebate is deducted from the assessed amount of tax payable, not from your income. If, because of your income level, you are not required to pay tax, the rebate does not take the form of a refund.

For further information about special circumstances under which the rebate may be claimed, read your Tax Pack or contact the Australian Taxation Office.

Income Tax And Social Security Payments

Detailed information about your taxation position should be obtained from the Australian Taxation Office.

TAXABLE PAYMENTS

All pensions, allowances and benefits are taxable except those listed below. Only the basic rate of benefit payment is taxable. Any additional payments, such as rent assistance or pharmceutical allowance, are not taxable. Family payments are not taxable.

If you have income other than a pension, allowance or benefit, your total income may exceed the tax threshold, so that you would become liable to pay tax. Social Security can then arrange for tax instalments to be deducted from the fortnightly payments. The Australian Taxation Office can advise how much tax should be deducted.

NON-TAXABLE PAYMENTS

These payments are free of tax:
- Family Payment.
- Child Disability Allowance.
- Disability Support Pension (except if you are over 65, male or 60, female).
- Wife Pension (if the wife is less than 60 and the husband less than 65).
- Carer Pension (if paid to a male less than 65 or to a female less than 60, when caring for a male less than 65 or a female less than 60).
- Rehabilitation Allowance.
- Sheltered Employment Allowance.
- Mobility Allowance.
- Telephone Allowance.
- Bereavement Allowance.
- Remote Area Allowance. The amount of the allowance is

deducted from any zone income tax rebate otherwise available to you.

- Double Orphan Pension
- Multiple Birth Allowance

STATEMENT OF EARNINGS AND GROUP CERTIFICATES

At the end of the financial year, Social Security issues a group certificate to people who have had tax instalments deducted from their pension, allowance or benefit. A statement of pension, allowance or benefit for the financial year is issued to all other clients.

PENSION REVIEWS

Pension reviews are conducted in two ways.

Every 12 weeks you will receive a pension review form. Details such as your current address, the occupants of your home, your bank accounts and any paid work you have are requested. You simply complete the form, sign it and return it, in person, to the DSS on the date specified. If you are unable to return the form by the due date, telephone the DSS and ask for an extension of time. Failure to return the form can result in the suspension of your payments.

Alternatively, a field assessor may visit you at your home:

- If you are unable to come to a regional office due to disability or illness, or
- To collect information to make sure that your payment is correct.

The field assessor may also make inquiries with your employer and other people to ensure that you are paid correctly. Don't forget, field assessors will always show their identification cards so you can be sure they are genuine. If you are concerned about answering questions at home, you can:

- Ask the field assessor to call back, perhaps enabling you to have another person there;

- Ask for time to think about your own questions and to have them written down;
- Ask to be interviewed at a regional office; or
- Choose to make a statement about the matters raised by the field assessor, instead of answering the questions on the spot.

You can ask for a copy of any form or statement that you have signed or a record of any interview you have had with the field assessor. (The same right applies to documents prepared in an office.) The field assessor can arrange this at the office and send you the copies.

Field assessors are not allowed into your house unless they are invited. Information about your rights should be given to you before the interview.

What You Must Tell Social Security

To ensure that you receive correct payments, you need to tell Social Security within 14 days if significant changes in your circumstances happen, such as:
- Your assets change significantly.
- You change your address (if you go overseas you must tell Social Security at least eight weeks before you leave).
- The amount of rent you pay changes or you stop paying rent.
- You start receiving maintenance or the amount you receive changes.
- You stop or start receiving Austudy or a similar Commonwealth Student Assistance Scheme payment.
- Your employment or income changes (if you start or give up work).
- Anything about your children changes (if they leave home, start work, turn 16 or other children come to live with you).
- You get back together with your former partner, marry or remarry or start living with a new partner in a marriage-like relationship.

The latter point is particularly important if you are receiving a sole parent pension. You are not eligible for this pension if you are living with your spouse or living in a marriage-like relationship. In certain circumstances, if you live with a person of the opposite sex who is not a close relative, social security could ask you for more information in order to check whether you should be getting the sole parent pension.

APPEALING AGAINST DEPARTMENT OF SOCIAL SECURITY DECISIONS

If you think a decision made about your Social Security entitlement is incorrect, there are several steps you can take:

- Discuss the matter at the local regional office with the original decision-maker.
- Request a review by an authorised review officer at an area office.
- Apply to the Social Security Appeals Tribunal (SSAT) for a review.
- Have the SSAT decision reviewed by the Administrative Appeals Tribunal.

You must request a review of a decision within three months of being advised of the original decision. Any arrears due from a reviewed decision will usually only be paid if the request was lodged within this three-month period.

Requesting a Review

The first step in the review process requires the original decision-maker to explain the disputed decision. This provides the opportunity to correct misunderstandings, to present new information or evidence and to have an incorrect decision changed quickly. If the original decision is not changed, you will be advised to discuss the matter with an authorised review officer. You will also be told about your right of appeal to the SSAT.

Authorised Review Officer

Authorised review officers are senior, expert staff located in area offices. They work independently of the regional offices and look at disputed decisions. They may:

- Set aside a decision and substitute a new one.
- Vary a decision.
- Affirm a decision.

  In order to do this, the authorised review officer will:

- Look at the information used by the original decision-maker.
- Where possible, discuss the matter with you by phone.
- Check whether any new, relevant information is available.
- Clear up any misunderstandings.
- Reconsider the original decision.
- Tell you the result in a letter explaining the reasons for the decision.

If you are still not satisfied, you may ask for a review of this decision by appealing to the Social Security Appeals Tribunal (SSAT). You can only make an appeal to the SSAT after you have seen the authorised review officer.

Social Security Appeals Tribunal (SSAT)

The Social Security Appeals Tribunal (SSAT) is an independent statutory authority, established as the first tier of external review of Social Security decisions. It aims to provide a mechanism of review that is fair, just, economical, informal and quick.

When reviewing a Social Security decision, the SSAT may affirm, vary or set aside a decision of the department. When it sets aside a decision, it substitutes a new one or sends the matter back to the department with directions or recommendations.

HOW TO APPLY

You may apply to the SSAT for a review of a decision by sending (or delivering) a written application to an office of the Tribunal, or to any Social Security regional office. Appeal forms are available from any Social Security or SSAT office. Applications may also be made by visiting or telephoning a Tribunal office. Applications are free of charge. The SSAT can pay reasonable travel and accommodation costs of applicants and will provide an interpreter when needed.

SSAT members are drawn from various backgrounds. They include lawyers, social and community welfare workers, medical practitioners and former Social Security officers.

The Tribunal has offices in all capital cities and sends panels to various regional centres from time to time. Applications are heard by a panel of three members. In medical cases, a medical member is added to the panel. Hearings are conducted in an informal manner. They are not like a court and it is not necessary to bring a lawyer. Hearings are in private but you may bring someone with you, who will also be allowed to talk to the Tribunal.

Within 14 days after deciding on the appeal, the SSAT must write, both to you and to the department, with its decision and reasons. Decisions made by the SSAT are binding. However, if either you or the department considers the SSAT's decision to be incorrect, you may each apply to the Administrative Appeals Tribunal (AAT) for a further review of the decision.

Administrative Appeals Tribunal (AAT)

The Administrative Appeals Tribunal (AAT) is a more formal body than the Social Security Appeals Tribunal (SSAT). Appeals to the AAT must be lodged in writing within 28 days of receiving a decision from the SSAT. Forms are available from the AAT Registry in each state.

TAX FILE NUMBERS (DATA MATCHING)

Data-matching means that Social Security asks people claiming or receiving payment from them to provide a tax file number (and the tax file number of their partner, where applicable). They check the information you give them against information already held by the

Australian Taxation Office and some other departments which pay benefits.

Some people are exempt from providing their tax file number, including those who are:

- In a nursing home or psychiatric hospital.
- Profoundly disabled.
- Living in a remote area or overseas.

OVERPAYMENTS

If you receive a Social Security payment, you have a responsibility to notify the department of any changes in your circumstances as soon as possible. Claim forms, income statements, review forms and notices issued clearly tell you what you are obliged to tell the department.

Failure to notify changes in income or other circumstances may result in an overpayment. The Social Security Act also provides for penalties or imprisonment if you misrepresent your circumstances or make false or misleading statements. You will be fully advised of the cause of any overpayment and details of the calculation will be supplied on request. In most instances, the department takes action to recover overpayments. A penalty is added to the amount of the debt, where a refund has not been received within three months. A maximum limit applies to the penalty.

The usual recovery methods are by:

- Withholding payment, if you are still due for any.
- Cash refund if you are no longer receiving payment.

Repayments can also be made in instalments through post offices, using a payment card issued by Social Security. The proportion of basic weekly rate of payment which is usually withheld in instalments is 14%. If this amount if too difficult to repay, the amount can be negotiated.

The department can also recover overpayments by:

- Garnishee of wages of employed debtors.
- Recovery directly from some bank or other financial accounts.
- Offsetting tax refunds against Social Security payments.

- Recovery against assets of the debtor (including real estate).

Negotiation is the department's basic debt recovery method and the rate of recovery is based on the debtor's capacity to repay. Formal powers and legal action are only used after negotiation of a reasonable repayment arrangement with the debtor has been tried but has failed.

PROTECTING YOUR PERSONAL INFORMATION

Much personal information about you is gathered in the course of your dealings with the Department of Social Security. To protect your rights, legislation provides certain safeguards.

Freedom Of Information

The Freedom of Information Act (FOI) gives you a general right of access to information held by Social Security. This information includes:

- Rules and guidelines used in the administration of the Social Security Act.
- Documents that Social Security holds about you.
- Any other documents in the possession of Social Security.
  The FOI Act also allows you to:
- Ask to have amended or annotated any incomplete, incorrect, out-of-date or misleading information held by Social Security about you.
- Appeal against any adverse decision under the Act.

REQUESTING RULES AND GUIDELINES

You do not need to make a written request to see any rule or guideline. If you want copies, there is no charge for the first 25 pages. For copies above the first 25 pages, there is a small charge per page.

Copies of complete manuals can be purchased from the Manuals Production Unit of the Department of Social Security in Canberra.

Copies of the Social Security Act can be purchased from Commonwealth Government bookshops in all capital cities.

REQUESTING PERSONAL INFORMATION OR OTHER DOCUMENTS

There are two other types of requests you can make under the FOI Act:

- Personal: a request to see your Social Security file or other documents about yourself.
- Non-personal: a request to see any other documents, such as documents relating to the functioning of the department.

To gain access to such documents, you should make a request in writing. You can make a request on a form called, 'I Want To See My File And Personal Documents'. This form is available from Social Security offices. Any such request has to be answered as soon as practicable and, in any event, not later than 30 days from when it is received.

If you receive or have received a pension, benefit or allowance, you will not have to pay to see your own documents, or to ask for a review of a decision to refuse you access to them. Professionals who want copies or are requesting a review are liable to an application fee and processing charges.

The Commonwealth Ombudsman

The Commonwealth Ombudsman is an independent person who can:

- Review the merits of decisions or policies.
- Investigate delays in making decisions.
- Investigate the conduct of government officials and poor administration.

Complaints to the Ombudsman can be made either by telephone or in writing. The Ombudsman cannot change a decision but can recommend that certain actions be taken. He or she can also report the results of any investigation to the Prime Minister and make special reports to Parliament.

The Right To Privacy

Under the Social Security Act, Social Security is required to collect and use personal and financial information about its clients. The Privacy Act sets detailed standards for the collection, storage, use and disclosure of such information by all Commonwealth Government agencies.

The Act determines what information is to be collected. It specifies that the information must be:

- Relevant.
- Necessary.
- Accurate.
- Up to date.
- Complete for the purpose of its collection.

The Act also determines how the information is collected. It must be collected:

- Fairly.
- Lawfully.
- Non-intrusively.

As a result of this legislation, when representatives of Social Security request personal information, they must explain:

- Why the information is needed.
- The legal authority for the request.
- Any circumstances where personal information may be passed on to another person or authority (the Act restricts the circumstances where this can happen).
- That the information will be kept safely and securely.
- How the information is to be used (it must be only for relevant purposes, with rare exceptions).
- What rights you have to see documents and computer records, to obtain copies and to ask to have personal records changed if they are wrong, out of date, incomplete, misleading or irrelevant.

The Privacy Commissioner has powers to investigate alleged breaches of the Privacy Act. He or she can issue binding directions to an agency and award damages to a complainant.

A FINAL WORD

The Federal Government in Australia is committed to providing social justice. People and families needing income support, or special assistance to achieve access to employment, can look to the Department of Social Security for help. While it may seem daunting to find your way around the system, and you may often feel frustration at being just one of many clients competing for the attention of the staff, they are there to help you. The key to success is you. You are responsible for deciding what you want to do. You need to be able to ask the questions which will produce the information you need. In the final analysis, you are the only one who can sweep away your own obstacles and move forward to a new life.

Directory

Parent Support Groups

NEW SOUTH WALES

Separated Parents Association for Readjustment (02) 588 3256
Parents Without Partners - State Office (02) 896 1888
Lone Parent Family Support (02) 982 5500
Single Parents of Australia (02) 642 0558
Christian Outreach Centre (02) 897 1455

VICTORIA

Parents Without Partners (03) 836 3211
Council of Single Mothers and their Children (03) 415 1171

QUEENSLAND

Lone Parent Self Action Group of Australia (07) 359 3700
Parents Without Partners (07) 844 8567
Lone Parent Club of Queensland (07) 252 7003

SOUTH AUSTRALIA

Parents without Partners (08) 232 3332
Centre of Personal Encounter (COPE) (08) 223 3433
SPARK Resource Centre Inc. (08) 347 1109

WESTERN AUSTRALIA

Parents Without Partners (09) 389 8350
Western Institute of Self Help (WISH) (09) 383 3188
Lone Parent Family Support Service (09) 389 8373
Lone Fathers family Support Service (09) 221 1668
Catholic Support Service (09) 221 1549

TASMANIA

Parents Without Partners (002) 240 897
Family Support Service (002) 347 725
Life Skills and Support Group (002) 781 660

AUSTRALIAN CAPITAL TERRITORY

Parents without Partners (ACT) (06) 248 6333
Lone Fathers Association Australia (06) 258 4216
Canberra One Parent Family Support (06) 247 4282

Refuges, Shelters & Emergency Accommodation

NEW SOUTH WALES

Women's Refuge Information Line (24 hours) (02) 560 5483
Women's Refuge Referral & Resource Centre (02) 560 1605
Homeless Persons Information Service (02) 265 9081

VICTORIA

Lifeline (24 hours) (03) 662 1000
Women's Refuge Referral Service (24 hours) (03) 329 8433;
  (freecall) (008) 015 188
Crisis Line (03) 329 0300

QUEENSLAND

Crisis Care (24 hours) (07) 365 9999
Women's Health, Information and Referral Service
  (freecall) (008) 017 382

SOUTH AUSTRALIA

Crisis Care (08) 232 3300

WESTERN AUSTRALIA

Crisis Care (24 hours) (09) 325 1111

TASMANIA

Hobart Women's Shelter (002) 346 323
Salvation Army, Ashfield House for Men (002) 284 520
St Joseph's (Centacare for Families) (002) 27 8705

NORTHERN TERRITORY

Dawn House Women's Shelter (089) 451 388
Darwin Aboriginal Shelter (089) 452 284

AUSTRALIAN CAPITAL TERRITORY

Beryl Women's Refuge (06) 247 5628
Caroline Chisholm Women's Refuge (06) 286 2173
Louisa Women's Refuge (06) 299 4799
Ainslie Village (men & women) (06) 257 5923
Toora Single Women's Shelter (06) 247 2438

Legal Advice & Services

NEW SOUTH WALES

Family Court of Australia:
  Office of the Chief Executive (02) 299 1577
  Sydney Registry (02) 226 7111
  Parramatta Registry (02) 893 5555
  Newcastle Registry (049) 261 255
  Wollongong Sub-Registry (042) 260 200
  Lismore (066) 218 977
  Albury (060) 218 944
  Dubbo (068) 858 460
Child Support Unit (02) 328 111; (008) 061 049
Child Support Agency (02) 131 272
Legal Aid Commission of NSW (02) 219 5000; also at
  Bankstown, Blacktown, Bondi Junction, Campbelltown,
  Fairfield, Hurstville, Leichhardt, Liverpool, Manly, Mount
  Druitt, Parramatta, Penrith, Ryde, Gosford, Lismore,
  Newcastle, Orange, Tamworth, Wagga Wagga and Wollongong

Community Legal Centres

Domestic Violence Advocacy Service (02) 637 3741
Women's Legal Resources Centre (02) 637 5012
Accommodation Rights Service (02) 281 3600
Blue Mountains Community Legal Centre (047) 824 155
Campbelltown Legal Centre (046) 282 042
Community Legal Centres Secretariat (02) 698 2401
Illawarra Legal Centre (042) 761 939
Inner City Legal Centre (02) 332 1966
Kingsford Legal Centre (02) 398 6366
Macquarie Legal Centre (02) 689 1777
Marrickville Legal Centre (02) 559 2166
Redfern Legal Centre (02) 698 7277
South West Sydney Legal Centre (02) 601 7777

Aboriginal Legal Services

Redfern (02) 699 9277; also at Armidale, Cowra, Grafton,
  Kempsey, Lismore, Moree, Newcastle West, Queanbeyan,
  Wagga Wagga, Walgett
South Coast Aboriginal Legal Service (044) 214 966; also at
  Bodalla, Wollongong
Western Aboriginal Legal Service Ltd, Dubbo (068) 826 966; also
  at Brewarrina, Broken Hill, Bourke (080) 873 233
Law Society of NSW (02) 220 0333 - legal advice centres are at
  Bankstown, Chatswood, Double Bay, Liverpool, Marrickville,
  Parramatta, Rockdale

VICTORIA

Family Court of Australia (03) 604 2900 - Counselling
  (03) 604 2800; Recorded Information (03) 1 1581
Dandenong (03) 767 6200
Bendigo (054) 423 888
Child Support Agency (03) 131 272
Legal Aid Commission of Victoria (03) 607 0234; also at Bendigo,
  Dandenong, Frankston, Geelong, Glenroy, Morwell, Preston,
  Ringwood, Sunshine

Community Legal Centres

Federation of Community Legal Centres (03) 419 2752, also at
  Broadmeadows, Caulfield East, Clifton Hill, Coburg, Doveton,
  Fitzroy, Flemington, Frankston North, Geelong, Monash-
  Oakleigh, Newport, North Melbourne, Nunawading and
  Western Suburbs, Springvale, St Kilda, Sunshine, West
  Heidelberg
Women's Legal Resources Group Limited (03) 416 0294
  (008) 133 302
Tenancy & Telephone Advice Service (03) 416 2577
Victorian Court Information and Welfare Network (03) 670 6977
Victorian Aboriginal Legal Service Co-Op (03) 419 3888; also at
  Bairnsdale; Robinvale
Dial-a-Law (03) 602 5000
Bar Council of Victoria (03) 608 7111
Citizens' Advice Bureau (03) 650 1062
Women's Information Referral Exchange (03) 654 6844;
  (008) 136 570

QUEENSLAND

Family Court of Australia - Brisbane (07) 233 8533
  Rockhampton (079) 31 6799
  Townsville (077) 229 333
  Cairns (070) 525 655
Child Support Unit - Brisbane (008) 077 066
Child Support Agency (07) 131 141
Legal Aid Commission (07) 238 3444; also at Cairns, Inala,
  Ipswich, Rockhampton, Southport, Toowoomba, Townsville,
  Woodridge, Bundaberg, Caboolture, Mackay

Community Legal Centres

Caxton Legal Centre (07) 254 1811
Community of Inala Legal Service (07) 372 7990
Maroochydore Neighbourhood Centre (074) 436 696

Petrie Community Legal Service (07) 205 6863
Citizen's Advice Bureau, Southport (075) 329 611
Toowoomba Community Legal Service (076) 383 950
South Brisbane Immigration & Community Legal Service
  (07) 846 3189
Women's Legal Service (07) 846 2066

Aboriginal Legal Services
Aboriginal and Torres Strait Islanders Corporation (07) 221 1448;
  also at Bundaberg, Charleville, Mackay, Oakley, Rockhampton,
  Townsville, Thursday Island, Toowoomba, Maryborough
West Queensland Aboriginal and Torres Strait Islanders
  Corporation for Legal Aid - Mt Isa (077) 437 448; also at
  Normanton, Mornington Island, Doomadgee
Tharpuntoo Legal Service, Cairns (070) 315 5633
Citizens' Advice Bureau (07) 221 4343
Queensland Law Society Inc. (07) 233 5888

SOUTH AUSTRALIA
Family Court of Australia (08) 205 2666
Child Support Unit (08) 131272
Collector of Maintenance (08) 231 0560
Legal Services Commission (08) 205 0111
Legal Advice (08) 205 0155; (008) 188 126; also at Elizabeth,
  Modbury, Noarlunga, Port Adelaide, Whyalla

Community Legal Centres
Bowden-Brompton (08) 346 9394
Marion Community Legal Service (08) 376 1300
Noarlunga (08) 384 5222
Norwood (08) 362 1199
Para Districts Community Legal Service (08) 281 6911
Parks Legal Service (08) 243 5555
Welfare Rights Centre (08) 223 4446

Aboriginal Legal Services

Aboriginal Legal Rights Movement (08) 211 8824; also at Ceduna,
  Murray Bridge, Port Augusta
Citizens' Advice Bureau (08) 212 4070
Law Society of SA (08) 231 9972

TASMANIA

Family Court of Australia Counselling Service - Hobart
  (002) 321 744; Launceston (003) 342 111
Tasmanian Legal Aid Commission (002) 346 544;
  Launceston (003) 317 088; Burnie (004) 315 622

Community Legal Centres

Hobart Community Legal Service (002) 345 988
Citizens' Advice Bureau (002) 440 671
Aboriginal Legal Service (002) 341 405
Tasmanian Aboriginal Centre (002) 348 311
Law Society of Tasmania (002) 344 133

NORTHERN TERRITORY

Family Court of Australia (089) 811 488
Northern Territory Legal Aid Commission (089) 814 799

Aboriginal Legal Services

Pitjantjatjara Council Legal Service, Alice Springs (089) 505 411
Central Australian Aboriginal Legal Aid Service (089) 522 933;
  also at Tennant Creek
North Australian Aboriginal Legal Aid Service (089) 815 266
Katherine Regional Aboriginal Legal Aid Service (089) 721 133
Law Society of the Northern Territory (089) 815 104

WESTERN AUSTRALIA

Family Court of Western Australia (09) 224 8222 - Counselling
  Service (09) 224 8248
Legal Aid Commission of WA (09) 261 6222; also at Fremantle,
  Midland

Community Legal Centres

Community Law Centre (09) 470 2676; also at Nedlands,
  Gosnells, North Perth (Migrant Resource Centre/East
  Victoria Park), Fremantle, West Perth (Youth Legal Service)
Citizens' Advice Bureau of Western Australia (09) 221 5711;
Fremantle (09) 335 4540; Rockingham (09) 527 6671

Aboriginal Legal Services

Aboriginal Legal Service, Perth (09) 265 6666; also at:
  Albany, Broome, Carnarvon, Derby, Geraldton, Halls Creek,
  Kalgoorlie, Kununurra, Laverton, Narrogin, Port Hedland,
  Roebourne
Law Society of WA Inc. (09) 221 3222

AUSTRALIAN CAPITAL TERRITORY

Family Court of Australia (06) 267 0511 - Counselling
  (06) 267 0620
Legal Aid Commission of the ACT (06) 243 3411

Community Legal Centres

Welfare Rights and Legal Centre (06) 247 2177
Aboriginal Legal Service (06) 257 6011
Citizens' Advice Bureau (06) 248 7988
Law Council of Australia (06) 247 3788
Law Society of the ACT (06) 247 5700

Social Security Appeals Tribunal

The SSAT can be contacted in all states and territories by writing
to GPO Box 9943 in your capital city, or by telephoning the
special number (008) 011 140 (or 008) 041 514 in the Australian
Capital Territory). You can also attend the SSAT office in your
capital city at the following addresses:
WA   - 1st Floor, Mt Newman House, 200 St Georges Terrace,
          Perth

NT   -   1st Floor, 80 Mitchell St, Darwin
TAS   -   1st Floor, 54 Victoria St, Hobart
ACT   -   2nd Floor, 4 Mort St, Canberra City
SA   -   12th Floor, 45 Grenfell St, Adelaide
QLD   -   6th Floor, 288 Edward St, Brisbane
VIC   -   14th Floor, 624 Bourke St, Melbourne
NSW   -   11th Floor, 157 Liverpool St, Sydney

Index